HOW TO LEAVE

HOW TO LEAVE

Quitting the City and
Coping with a New Reality

ERIN CLUNE

BLOOMSBURY PUBLISHING

NEW YORK · LONDON · OXFORD · NEW DELHI · SYDNEY

BLOOMSBURY PUBLISHING
Bloomsbury Publishing Inc.
1385 Broadway, New York, NY 10018, USA

BLOOMSBURY, BLOOMSBURY PUBLISHING, and the Diana logo are trademarks
of Bloomsbury Publishing Plc

First published in the United States 2018
Copyright © Erin Clune, 2018

Some of the names, locations, and identifying characteristics have been changed to
protect the privacy of individuals portrayed in this book. Some people and stories are
composites.

Bloomsbury Publishing Plc does not have any control over, or responsibility for, any
third-party websites referred to or in this book. All internet addresses given in this book
were correct at the time of going to press. The author and publisher regret any
inconvenience caused if addresses have changed or sites have ceased to exist, but can
accept no responsibility for any such changes.

ISBN: HB: 978-1-63286-854-1; eBook: 978-1-63286-856-5

LIBRARY OF CONGRESS CATALOGING-IN-PUBLICATION DATA

Names: Clune, Erin, author.
Title: How to leave : quitting the city and coping with
a new reality / Erin Clune.
Description: New York : Bloomsbury, 2018.
Identifiers: LCCN 2017055429| ISBN 9781632868541 (hardback) |
ISBN 9781632868565 (ebook)
Subjects: LCSH: Clune, Erin. | City and town life—United States. |
Community life—United States. | Regional disparities—United States. |
Moving, Household—United States. | Adjustment (Psychology)
Classification: LCC HT123 .C558 2018 | DDC 307.760973—dc23
LC record available at https://lccn.loc.gov/2017055429

2 4 6 8 10 9 7 5 3 1

Typeset by Westchester Publishing Services
Printed and bound in the U.S.A. by Berryville Graphics Inc., Berryville, Virginia

To find out more about our authors and books visit www.bloomsbury.com and
sign up for our newsletters.

Bloomsbury books may be purchased for business or promotional use. For information on
bulk purchases please contact Macmillan Corporate and Premium Sales Department at
specialmarkets@macmillan.com.

for Mike

CONTENTS

Dear Reader   ix

PART ONE: DECIDING TO GO

1. Making It There   3

2. Stop the Gerbil Wheel, I Wanna Get Off!   20

3. Nobody Leaves Without a Fight   49

PART TWO: SETTLING IN

4. It's the End of the World as You Know It, and
   You Have Questions   71

5. Culture Shock Is Real   86

6. The Targets of My Discontent   102

PART THREE: LEARNING TO ADAPT

7. Let the Adjustment Games Begin!   121

8. The World Is Your Oyster, but It's Not
   Necessarily Your Clam   149

9. One Step Forward, and Back You Go!   165

PART FOUR: MASTERY

10. Mastering the Art of Artichokes 183

11. Telling the Po-Po What They Need to Know 195

12. Living (Parts of) the Suburban Dream 209

13. Losing Your Kids in the Woods 219

14. Doorknob Confessions 232

Afterword 251

Acknowledgments 254

DEAR READER

This book is about leaving. It's not about leaving your husband for a woman. Or leaving the country because the wrong candidate was elected. If you want to do either of those things, I hope you get a good lawyer. And a different book. This book is about the kind of leaving where—because of work or family or health care or some other real-life reason—you decide to leave the fabulous and familiar place you call home and move someplace else.

Moving is traumatic under the best of circumstances. It's even more emotionally fraught when you still love your home and can't imagine living anywhere else. I felt that way about New York City. Leave?! It has everything! High-rises. High fashion. Flash mobs. Actual mobs. Identity pride parades. Bike-delivered food. Tiny trash tornadoes on a windy day. That man who roams around midtown with a cat on his head. It's the unique, quirky aspects of daily life in the city that New Yorkers cherish most. Let me ask you this: Did you ever stand in Times Square on New Year's, freezing your ass off for ten hours because your boyfriend said you had to do it, just once? If the answer is yes, I hope you broke up with that guy. Nobody has to do that, not even once.

I use New York as an example because it was *my* beloved home. But as this book demonstrates, people have special connections to so many other places. No matter where you live, or in what time zone you watch New Year's on TV, you can relate to Frank Sinatra's triumphant words: "If I can make it there, I'll make it anywhere!" Maybe your version of making it was cooking vegan spring rolls and taking long hikes in Seattle. Maybe it was eating barbecue and going to zombie film festivals in Austin. Or maybe you followed your heart to Denver to spend every weekend shredding it on the slopes then sitting in traffic on I-70. Maybe the traffic wasn't part of the dream. The point is, when you find the place where you find yourself, you never want to leave.

Until you do. At which point, everyone who ponders leaving their favorite place suddenly starts to freak out: Wait, can I really make it anywhere? After two decades in San Francisco, does *anywhere* include a tract housing community in Oklahoma City? After ten years in Minneapolis, does *anywhere* include a gated golf community in a quiet suburb of Boise? For New Yorkers: Isn't everywhere in flyover country—with the exception of a few award-winning restaurants in Chicago—pretty much always asleep? WTF, Frank Sinatra! Does Boise even have suburbs?!

I'm not sure about the answer to that last question, but the overall answer is still yes. You *can* make it anywhere, even if that place is somewhere in Idaho, with its incomprehensibly small Canadian border and its mythological suburbs. You *can* leave a place that makes you feel alive and relocate to a place that is routinely described as *livable*. How do I know this? Because after living in New York for almost twenty years—minus one disturbing year in Rhode Island—I moved back to the Midwest with a husband, two children, better hair, and exactly two rooms of furniture. And I survived to write a book about it.

After combing through decades of largely reliable memories, I felt compelled to turn my personal story into a practical coping guide, designed for anyone who may be facing a new reality. Countless social scientists have studied the intricate emotional factors involved in moving. Most of that research, while probably very interesting, does not appear in this book. Instead, it's inspired by the wisdom that I've been acquiring most of my life. Like, since I was a baby. Maybe even since I was a fetus, preparing to migrate south. Most important, I grounded this book in my own experience of leaving New York and moving back to my hometown of Madison, Wisconsin, a town so pleasant and livable I couldn't wait to get the hell out. As a teenager, I once stomped out to the back porch, where my mom and her friends were drinking iced tea, and boasted that I would rather die than grow old in Wisconsin drinking iced tea on a porch. *Great,* my mom thought, rolling her eyes, *how soon can you start packing?*

Eventually, I did move away. After going to college in California, then working for a few years in Washington D.C., I landed in New York City. It was pretty different from my parents' back porch. For one thing, it was bigger. Three of its five boroughs, put together, contain more people than the entire state of Wisconsin. More people visit Times Square on a busy day than officially reside in my entire hometown! Also, most people in New York don't even have porches. They have stoops.

Yet if that was the full story, I wouldn't be here, promising to fix your life. The truth is that I barely escaped that tragic, iced tea–drinking fate, only to find myself back on the same exact porch twenty years later. I still don't like iced tea. I'd always just rather have coffee. But the process of returning has taught me some new things. One is that people sometimes need support when they move. Moving is not as mathematically straightforward as, say, lowering the carb ratio in your diet, or losing your baby weight. Most women I know just put that little walking bracelet on and the pounds fall right off. And everyone knows how good statistics are at changing irrational behavior. Ever told a heavy smoker how many more years they'd live if they just stopped sucking on those tar sticks? It's like a magic nicotine patch made of numbers! Right? But moving away, and coping with the reality of your life in a new place, can be a slightly more complex endeavor.

Don't get me wrong: This program is not a panacea. It should not be taken in place of lifesaving medication. It won't cure your acid reflux or help you navigate through Paducah, Kentucky, during heavy rainfall. Also, this book contains very few, if any, pithy motivational phrases like *Life is an adventure*. I'm not sure how people who say things like that actually have friends. If anyone had said that to me when I was trying to figure out how to leave New York, I would've punched them. Or at least posted a throw-up emoji on their timeline.

Rather than inspiring you, this book will help you see the world around you more clearly so you can manage your expectations. You need to know that even if you always use the GPS, you will still sometimes get lost out there in the wilds of the suburbs. Like when you're driving in the sticks, looking for a corn maze, and suddenly find yourself on an unmarked road because the Silicon Valley dude who programmed the satellite thinks everyone in Wisconsin is Amish. You need to know that outside of large urban areas, they have very few billboards, exactly *not any* of which feature David Beckham in his underwear. You'll be lucky to see a group of fully clothed middle-aged men standing awkwardly above a caption that reads HOLIDAY GREETINGS FROM THE MANAGEMENT TEAM AT YOUR FRIENDLY NEIGHBORHOOD CREDIT UNION. And you need to know that you probably can't just catch a taxi. You can maybe order a Lyft, and in twenty-five minutes, someone you went to high school with will swing by in a flatbed truck on his way to a meat raffle. At which point, you may decide to tag along, because duh, meat raffles are everything.

I'm exaggerating, slightly. It's not like your new place is going to be a windowless military pod in Afghanistan! Unless that's where you did decide to move, in which case, I might suggest turning off that GPS. For everyone else, you can do this! My program will assure you that just because you once found yourself in the big city of your dreams doesn't mean you still need that place to feel true or whole. Embracing your new reality for what it is—a simpler life filled with kind, hardworking people who value nature, community, and large cuts of nicely marbled meat— will take some time. Finding people who get you will also take time. Meeting people who are as loud and outspoken as you are will *definitely* take time. Depending on how far away you move, in fact, many of these people may turn out to be geese. If that happens, I advise you to turn tail and walk away ASAP, because those birds do not play. They flew all the way down here from Canada to hatch those fuzzy little duck babies, and if you come anywhere near them, those bitches will *bite* you.

PART ONE

Deciding to Go

Chapter 1

MAKING IT THERE

NOTHING IN LIFE is more terrifying than having to leave your favorite city in the world to move to a place where, relatively speaking, nobody wants to live. That's how I felt, anyway, as I drove up to the suburban condo that my husband's new company had rented for us. Mike had moved three months before me and the kids. Now, in June, we were finally joining him. And he had warned me!

"The neighborhood is kind of rural," Mike had said on the phone, when I was still packing up our apartment. "But there's a coffee shop right down the road!"

"A coffee shop?" I said. "One?" I think I heard him nod.

Even though this area wasn't residentially developed when I was a kid, I could imagine the place he described. The condo was just on the outskirts of town, and in Wisconsin, the transition from town to country happens pretty fast. One minute you're picking up a sack of pistachios at a gourmet nut shop and the next you're on a dark two-lane highway and can't find an open gas station.

The condominium complex was named after a wilderness feature. Like, the Waterside. Or Pleasant View. Or Wind Sheer

Lane? Okay, I don't remember the name. Truthfully, I couldn't remember it most of the time I was living there. Clichés are too easy to forget. I feel like developers only use nature branding in order to distract residents from the fact that they're moving to the middle of nowhere. Rather than surrender to their false advertising, I just called it the "ugly condo." I could have called it the "scary condo." It was right across the street from a corn-field and if you saw *Children of the Corn*, you know what I'm saying.

The condo itself was clean. It wasn't infested with rats or roaches or rednecks. Well, there were a few rednecks. But Mike didn't share my skepticism. He thought the condo was fine because it had a parking lot, a little workout room with a tiny TV, and a washer/dryer *inside* the unit, which, by New York standards, was some luxury shit. Mostly, Mike just didn't spend much time there. He'd been living by himself for three months, and he spent almost every day at work. To him, the ugly condo was just an affordable development built for easy commuting into town, filled with a lot of other residents who were just like him, except they didn't treat the washer/dryer like a five-star amenity.

I don't think petty looked particularly good on me, but that's what I was wearing. After months of good-bye lunches, farewell dinners, final book clubs, and parting coffees, I'd jammed most of our possessions into a storage unit and moved a thousand miles away from almost everyone I knew in the universe. The day before I landed in the cornfield, my bestie, Tara, threw a party for us at her apartment on the east side. It was an intimate gathering of old friends, longtime colleagues, and Tara's French bulldog, Carlos. Afterward, Tara took Carlos for a walk in the rain, slipped on a wet curb, and shattered the left side of her face. It really sucked for her. But, since she didn't tell me about it at the time, I felt 100 percent sorry only for myself.

My first morning in Wisconsin, I sat in the furnished living room, surrounded by piles of badly labeled boxes, asking myself the same three questions: 1) What the *hell* am I going to do out here every day with two toddlers? 2) What time will Mike be done with work? And 3) Which one of these fucking boxes has the electric wine bottle opener?! After a few days, I picked my ass up off the floor and went to the coffee shop. Unlike in New York, going "right down the road" meant carrying both kids out to the car, strapping them into their seats, and driving half a mile to the nearest strip mall. In the afternoons, we'd drive into town to find a park or something. Once in a while, we drove to see my parents. But since they hadn't retired yet, visiting Gramma and Grampa usually meant driving across town to babysit my own kids in an empty house—the exact house in which my sister once stuck a piece of chicken up her nose and forgot about it, my baby brother filched my razor and shaved off all his arm hair, and my dad chopped off his thumb with a wood guillotine. Great job, family!

Was I *suffering*? Oh, please. I'm quasi-depressive and emotionally needy, but I'm not a total dick. We had the financial means to move, which a lot of people don't have. I chose not to find a paying job that first year so I could help transition the kids. We weren't moving to get away from gun violence or a natural disaster or political repression. So, first-world problems. Still, no matter who you are, it's hard to be in a strange place with no friends, no schedule, no permanent home, and no place to walk but a creepy cornfield full of child zombies. We lasted barely a month out there before renting a place closer to town.

What I wish I'd known at the time—apart from when my parents would be home to babysit—was how common my feelings were! Technically speaking, I was alone. Nobody was there to distract me during those long days in the condo, while my kids weren't napping. And that was probably for the best, because I was no fun to be around anyway. But I wasn't alone in terms of my experience. All across America were thousands of people like me who had just relocated and were walking their kids around broken-down shopping malls trying to find an electric wine opener and wondering why everyone else was smiling.

I read a few essays around that time, mostly by other New Yorkers. I don't know if New Yorkers are especially creative—or especially self-centered—but they do write about their experiences a lot. I get that. Leaving New York is still one of my favorite topics of discussion, along with what cocktail to make and whether my orange cat has the fat gene. I'm part of a vast echo chamber of people who spent most of their adult lives in New York and will probably spend the rest of their adult lives whining about it.

Why didn't I know that the emotional toll of moving was so universal? Although people move to different places, for myriad reasons, the overall narrative is remarkably common. Did I miss their stories because they moved down to Miami, bought an ornamental neck snake, and fell off the grid? Did they leave Los Angeles to escape air pollution, only to be snuffed out by a noxious suburban microclimate of SUV exhaust and lawn pesticides? I've heard rumors of people who tried to leave Chicago and fell into a sinkhole underneath the Mercantile Exchange. They might still be down there craving puffy pizza, poor dummies.

But for everyone else: Good news! Having survived my relocation, I resolved to track down other stories and incorporate them into my program. One of these people was a woman in her late twenties—I'll call her "Ruby"—who had likewise lived in New York City for many years. She still very much loved it there when her husband got a promotion opportunity in Scottsdale, Arizona. Ruby and her husband decided to take a leap of faith, thinking they would stay for a limited number of years. Like four, maybe. Tops. They only grasped how tough the adjustment would be, however, when their real estate agent called and said she had found them the "perfect house."

During a tour of this dream home, the agent pointed over the fence to the open desert, explained that it backed up to Native American land, and promised they'd "have desert sunsets forever." At which point, Ruby started to have a panic attack. She wasn't worried about corn zombies. After all those years living in New York, she was just so "overwhelmed by the nothingness," she actually felt claustrophobic. Technically, I guess it was reverse claustrophobia, but I'm not here to police anyone's lingo. The point is that when she stared at that beautifully preserved indigenous land, all she could think about was how lonely she felt.

I also learned the story of "Hillary," who left Los Angeles after eleven years when her wife lost her job. Because her wife was from New Zealand, they decided to move there. In their first apartment Down Under, Hillary set up her home office and put her desk by a window that overlooked a park. As she gazed outside one day, trying to find the right word for a sentence, it suddenly dawned on her that the pohutukawa trees, "while stunning, had no mammals" in them. It's not like she was a chipmunk whisperer or had nursed an injured field mouse back to health in California. It was just an idiosyncratic detail that triggered her loneliness. Bereft of mini-mammals, she cried for two days.

We'll talk about coping in later chapters. But right now, we have more fundamental questions to answer. Like, why is it so difficult for us to leave places we call home? Why is it even difficult for us to leave places that have become financial, emotional, or actual sinkholes? Well, unraveling this Gordian knot is a bit like figuring out why anyone still goes into the fun house at a carnival, when it's really just a room full of weird mirrors. Human behavior can be puzzling. Consider these two completely contradictory rationales for why people don't leave, say, New York.

THEY BELIEVE NEW YORK IS THE BEST PLACE IN THE WORLD.

Ask anyone who's lived in New York for an extended period of time, on purpose, and they will testify that New York is the best place in the world. They love New York so much, they actually talk about the city in romantic terms. Like it's a partner. Or a *lover*. That word is gross. Especially when applied to actual humans. But the love is real. I love New York even more than I love the South of France, and I would personally throw an

actual human lover under an actual bus for the right vintage of
Côtes du Rhône.

Converts aren't the only zealots; people born and raised in
New York give the same glowing reviews. Here's what Cari
Luna of *Salon* wrote, for example, about her painful decision to
quit New York and move to Portland to raise chickens: "You're
in the center of the universe, right? And you're so in love with
the city that the sight of the Manhattan skyline as you ride the
Q train over the bridge at night is enough to make you weep."
Deep thoughts—and that was before the Second Avenue line
was even finished!

While I can't recall ever weeping on the Q train, I understand her cosmology. The first time I went to New York, it was
the summer after my freshman year of college. I'd spent most
of that summer back in Wisconsin, living with my parents and
younger siblings and working at a mom-and-pop Italian grocery.
My co-workers were a fun-loving crew of underachievers, which
in Madison is a euphemism for stoners. The one exception was
Fran, an older gal who ran the grocery register. She kept a wet
sponge next to her money drawer, and one day she told me why.
"For years," Fran explained, "I just licked my finger to grab the
money. Then one night, at a strip club, I saw how many of those
dollar bills got stuck in between a stripper's butt cheeks, or
worse." I didn't ask Fran why she went to strip clubs. Or what
worse meant. But that was literally the only thing she ever said
to me, so I took that life lesson and walked away.

As educational as that grocery job was, nothing that summer
compared to my first trip to New York. I went out with a whole
group to visit a college roommate who lived in New Jersey.

Our roommate's dad—a super nice guy who I remember as looking exactly like James Gandolfini—drove us into the city. We started at Katz's Delicatessen. That meat blew my mind, and I grew up eating a lot of meat. The Vikings didn't get all the way to the Upper Midwest eating trail mix, bitches! But in my hometown, exactly zero Jewish delis had kitschy signs hanging from the ceiling that said things like SEND A SALAMI TO YOUR BOY IN THE ARMY. And I think that's because *salami* and *army* don't rhyme in Wisconsin. Also, my hometown had only one Jewish deli.

We walked all over the West Village and the Lower East Side. We wandered down Houston Street, hit the flea market on Broadway, and crisscrossed through SoHo. I've had to piece that trip together in retrospect, from pictures. I had no idea where I was; I was just following James Gandolfini. But I have never forgotten how beautiful it all looked, in real time. Wide streets. Historic factory buildings with soaring arched windows. Vast, painted brick walls. It was a lot like Chicago, where I was born, but so much bigger, so much more artistic, so much more full of mean salespeople who don't let tourists use the bathroom.

Before going there, I'd seen New York only on TV: *All in the Family. The Jeffersons. Welcome Back, Kotter.* I knew these sitcoms were fictional, but I could also tell from watching them that New Yorkers were brazen, blunt, and sometimes outrageous people. Growing up in the less diverse, more polite culture of Wisconsin, these personality traits charmed me. Even the crankiness—while it sometimes hurt my feelings and occasionally scared the living crap out of me—appealed to me. I don't know if I wanted to crush it or join it. But either way, it was a challenge I couldn't resist.

Finally, at the age of twenty-four, I moved to New York. There I was in the big city, with my whole life—minus those first twenty-four years—laid out in front of me. Like so many people who move to cool cities to start their first jobs (or, in my case, start graduate school), I went to New York as a single, starry-eyed debutante. The big city had seduced me, and now it would deflower me, too—or at least, that part of me that was naïve, innocent, and sheltered. Over the next fifteen years, New York expanded my horizons. It redefined my comfort zone. It made me feel alive in a way I had never felt before, and not just when I was jacked up on speedball cocktails made of SSRIs, oxygen facial vapors, and bus exhaust.

My coming-of-age story was written in New York, but no matter where you move, a new place exposes you to exciting new risks and challenges. At the age of twenty-seven, a woman named "Jamie" moved from Buffalo to Washington, D.C., for her first full-time job as a Latin teacher, because she was passionately committed to teaching children a dead language. As a parting gift, her eighty-year-old grandfather gave her two cast-iron pans, one six-inch, the other ten-inch. She tried to refuse, explaining that she already had cookware. They aren't for cooking, he told her. They're for "personal security." He instructed her to keep the small one in the car and the large one under her bed, in case she got jumped. Jamie arrived in D.C. with a heavier heart, and much, much heavier luggage.

For young people with minimal real-world responsibility, cities can be a blast. I loved New York because it pulsed with activity and bustled with humanity. I'd never lived in a place where the cranes were taller, the old people were crustier, or the Thanksgiving floats were quite so deadly in a strong gust of wind. It's a people-watching paradise, with absorbing human dramas everywhere you look. Kids on scooters being pulled by their moms. Investment bankers on cocaine yelling at their lawyers. Dogs in strollers. Queens in drag. I moved to New York to get a formal education, but I stayed for the informal one. I'm pretty sure it was either that, the fresh egg creams, or the intoxicating smell of steaming-hot urine that floats up through the sidewalk grates all summer long.

For many people, rejecting a place this spectacular is like turning your back on a fairy tale just because there is one wicked witch. And when I say that, I'm not talking about that old woman who wanders around Union Square Park stomping the life out of pigeons. I'm speaking metaphorically, about hardship. And this brings me to the other major reason people have a hard time leaving a place as fabulous as New York.

IT'S TAKEN *FOREVER* TO MAKE IT THERE, AND THEY CAN'T GET THOSE YEARS BACK.

Some people fall in love with New York, and stay for a really long time, but then—like that boyfriend who makes you feel special because he laughs at everything you say, until you realize he's just been stoned the whole time—get sick of its bullshit. Every place has its own bullshit. But even when New York's bullshit has beaten them down to the point where they don't notice the smell of urine anymore, even when it's emanating from someplace on their own body, they refuse to break it off.

The *Onion*, a satirical newspaper, alluded to this fighting spirit when it called New York a "massive, trash-ridden hellhole that slowly sucks the life out of every one of its inhabitants." Is it a coincidence that the *Onion* actually started in my hometown and then followed me to New York? Totally. But there's another reason this gallows humor resonates with me. In the city, it's a survival trait. As the great Indian spiritual leader Mahatma Gandhi once reportedly said: *If I didn't have a sense of humor, I would have committed suicide a long time ago.* That Gandhi. What a crack-up!

Some New Yorkers become so miserable, they actually can't joke about it anymore. Remember Cari Luna's account of weeping for joy on the Q train? Well, she also wrote this: "Or maybe you're crying because you're tired from working your barely living-wage publishing job and then doing freelance work all night to cover your rent; or maybe you're crying because New York is an absolutely brutal place to be a single woman; or maybe you're crying because you're in your 20s and it's all so beautiful and big and overwhelming, the city spread out before you like that." I'm not a comedy expert, but that's some unfunny shit right there.

So, why don't people who feel this much ambivalence or downright misery about New York, or wherever they reside, just pick up . . . and *leave?* Some folks might wonder, *Can't they scrape together enough overtime to rent a moving van and drive it to Omaha?* Nebraska may not be the center of the universe, or have a publishing industry, but wouldn't you save a lot, just on Visine and Kleenex alone?

The short answer, in my humble opinion, is that they don't want New York to win. They've driven through the Lincoln Tunnel so often that when they add it up, they realize they've spent three full years being angry under the Hudson River.

They've taken the subway so many times, they know exactly where to stand so they can't be blocked out—or shoved onto the third rail—when the train arrives. The logistical mastery of the city matters. New Yorkers know their way around it; they know which areas are safe, and which bodegas are open late at night for a loosie. Commuting to work in New York, every day, is a version of the Kobayashi Maru. Are they supposed to survive that no-win situation, day after day, then suddenly give up and move to a town filled with patient people who wait their turn? It's the principle of the thing. They shed a lot of tears weathering all those tests, challenges, and changes to the Q line—and they want them to count!

When people talk about *making it* in New York, they aren't talking about a place where the livin' is easy. By the standard of that old tune, it's almost never summertime in New York. It's more like a dystopian reality show in which everyone is dropped onto the same small island, to compete for affordable housing. For as long as I can remember, people have been trying to figure out how to deal with gentrification in the outer boroughs. And I'm here for that concern. Because as long as millionaires are voting everyone else off the fancy island, those old neighborhoods in Brooklyn are going to keep getting more expensive.

Not just in Brooklyn, but in the whole New York area. A recent study of black millennials found that housing costs were driving highly educated professionals—who liked living in New York and had built very successful careers—to southern cities like Atlanta. Not only does this city have the reputation for being a black mecca, but a state attorney can afford a four-bedroom town house in a good school district in Atlanta, which is not a New York fact pattern.

So many people stick around, though, and live with their ambivalence. It's even possible to love New York and hate it in the same day! One minute, you're cruising up Amsterdam Avenue, humming a Beyoncé song, dreaming about a mushroom burger from Shake Shack. Momentarily, it starts to rain. Your humming is drowned out by a jackhammer at one of New York's constant construction sites, and when you turn the corner to get in a line that stretches around the block, you step right into a pile of human-size shit. Two feet in front of you, you spot a junkie pulling up his pants. Gandhi would obviously find that scene hilarious. But it just ruined your mood.

When I first moved to the city, a guy told me it would take at least a year of living in New York before I even *noticed* how miserable I was. That guy had lived in New York for ten years already. He still seemed pretty damn miserable to me. But I knew what he meant. When daily life is that cutthroat and chaotic, you live in survival mode for a while and make a mental note to check in with your feelings when the numbness wears off.

New Yorkers are by no means the only people who experience urban trial by fire. I met a pediatrician named "Mandy" who moved to Seattle for her husband's medical fellowship. Mandy remembers the horror of her family's first preschool picnic like it was yesterday. As a native midwesterner, she'd assumed the picnic would be a potluck. Mindful of how many people in Seattle were vegans, gluten avoiders, and otherwise restricted eaters, she made a big organic fruit salad. They "arrived to find a fifty-year-old braless mom breastfeeding her three-year-old," and everyone else "eating dinners in plastic-free bento boxes or cardboard Whole Foods containers." Her family sat, despondently, eating their fruit for dinner. With their fingers. After several of these cultural bloopers, Mandy finally decided that Seattleites just don't share food—unless it's salmon, "which is present at every gathering." For Mandy, figuring out when to share—and when to hoard your fruit salad—was part of "making it" in Seattle. Once you know the rules, you start to feel like you belong.

It's also hard to imagine leaving your friends—a support network that may have taken years and years to build—just because you can't find a nice apartment. When I first arrived in New York, I had a bunch of childhood friends who were there already and helped me to acclimate. Historians have a word for this kind of demographic clumping. It's called *chain migration*. This historical pattern explains why Polish people clustered in Greenpoint, Brooklyn, why religious Jewish people gathered in Flatbush, and why almost everyone in Carroll Gardens in the nineties was either a member of the Italian mafia or an improv comedian from Wisconsin.

After a few years, I lost all these friends in a breakup and had to build my support network from scratch. In the early days, though, my Wisconsin crew helped me get a studio apartment on the ground floor of a tenement building on Sullivan Street. Except for the fact that it was microscopic, cost more than half my monthly income, and was infested with water bugs, it was *perfect*. My next-door neighbor in that building was an unemployed actress from Long Island.

"Water bugs," she explained to me, "are what New Yorkers call *yuge* cockroaches. Some people will try to tell you they're a different species. They definitely aren't." I don't know where my neighbor got her entomological information. But I didn't care. As far as I was concerned, a bug had to be *really* disgusting if New Yorkers—who typically get off on shocking each other with verbal zingers—use a soothing aquatic euphemism to describe them.

And believe me, that apartment was disgusting. It had this pond in the courtyard, about three feet from my studio window, which would have been a bucolic-looking nature feature, except that it was never cleaned. The only people who truly loved the pond were the Hells Angels. Their favorite watering hole was right down the block and after the bar closed, they'd bust through our front gate to terrorize the turtles.

The "water bugs" were more like an indoor nature feature. All night, I would lie in my bed and listen to them clicking across the hardwood floor, like foot soldiers plotting a bug revolt. Everyone in New York knows that their walls are basically filled—floor to ceiling—with roaches. But they live in the walls, you tell yourself, and mostly stay in there. They're afraid of you. This comforting self-talk worked like a charm until the night I decided to take a bath in my 150-year-old bathtub and a water bug the size of a Twinkie plopped out of the faucet onto my naked stomach. And that, dear Reader, was the last time I ever took a bath in New York City.

ONCE WE FIND ourselves in a place, we feel like we belong there, and we're independent and free. This is a story about identity, and sense of place, and it's familiar to so many of us, no matter where we live. One thing Mandy really loved about Seattle—other than the salmon—was "riding in an elevator with one or more people in complete and total silence." I get it. Big city dwellers take comfort in anonymity. Not having to chat with strangers about bullshit is one of the fringe benefits of overcrowding. Even celebrities in New York expect to be left alone, although that doesn't always happen. I ran into Wallace Shawn once, for example, in a restaurant in NoHo. He was sitting alone, going through a backlogged stack of newspapers and magazines. I talked to him for fifteen minutes before it dawned on me that he probably went there to be alone. But that was an authentic New York moment, too. Because Wallace Shawn is a fixture. Everyone, if they stay in New York long enough, will eventually fuck up Wallace Shawn's day.

You go to the city and soon enough, you are part of a larger romantic narrative. *The urban success story.* You can now cross a busy street against a light without really caring whether an oncoming cab runs you over. You're a superpedestrian who can walk ten blocks north and two avenues west and never once stop your forward motion. You are a savvy subway rider who can get on a crowded train and know instinctively not to take that empty seat, because within a few minutes, the guy sitting next to it will burp a bunch of times, then start to dry heave into his backpack. From across the train, you observe that his eyeglasses are just empty plastic frames and his shirt wasn't meant to be sleeveless.

In grad school, I spent so many hours at the main research library on Forty-Second Street that it practically felt like home. It was like my own private palace, with a basement full of secrets and a majestic reading room full of men whose hands were under the table, doing God knows what. It took me a year just to figure out how to use the microfilm machines, and two more to figure out how to order a book from the stacks so it would come up right after lunch. Leave? *Now?* And do what? Eat mandatory wankloads of salmon in Seattle?

Whether it's love or hate or a surf-and-turf platter of both, people have lots of reasons not to leave their homes. It's hard to do, whether you are living life to its fullest or barely living at all. So maybe you will just stay. And that's fine. But if you think you have reached the point where you are ready to take that leap of faith, to transcend your mental and logistical barriers and ultimately say good-bye, then I have more words for you in chapter two.

Chapter 2

STOP THE GERBIL WHEEL, I WANNA GET OFF!

FOR WHATEVER REASON, you have come to realize that you're dissatisfied with your current situation. Something is pushing you, or pulling you, and in the midst of this emotional tug-of-war in which you are the chunky rope, you have found yourself pondering the colossal question: Should you leave?

There isn't an easy answer. These are tough times, Reader, and this is a tough chapter. But I am here for you. To help you step across that line—to your bright future, not over a cliff like Yosemite Sam—we shall begin with some thoughts on failure.

HAVE I FAILED?

Experts agree that moving is one of the most stressful things a person can do. On the official stress meter, it ranks right up there with a family death, divorce, and trying to strap a screaming toddler into a car seat with a five-point harness. And in times of acute psychological stress, we often become irrationally self-blaming and needlessly self-destructive. Remember this when you start asking yourself if you are ready to leave—unless you've been living on that barge of New York garbage that has been floating around the Atlantic for the past twenty years. If you're experiencing stress and disorientation about leaving *that* place, you probably just have lead poisoning. You should totally leave. Right now. Just go.

For everyone else, however, the decision to leave can make you feel like you are giving up, being rejected, or, worst of all: *failing*. Like you gave it your best shot at the wedding but didn't catch the bouquet. Like you tried for that Super Bowl ring but all you got was another debilitating concussion. Like you ran for the highest office in the land as the first woman candidate from a major party, won the popular vote by almost three million, and still lost to a deranged carnival barker whose kids all look like fun-house distortions of Draco Malfoy.

Writer Adam Sternbergh once discussed the emotional phenomenon of people leaving New York City. At that time, droves of New Yorkers were reportedly selling off their midcentury modern furniture and moving upstate. They were like pioneers, but much less self-sufficient. The problem, Sternbergh wrote, "is you can't simply leave New York—you have to *quit* New York. You have to admit to yourself and the world that you're packing it in, calling it a day, turning out the lights."

I think midcentury modern furniture is ugly, but I feel that dark metaphor. Extracting yourself from a cool city like New York isn't like pulling your kids out of a play-based preschool where everyone gets a participation ribbon for building a cool tower with blocks. It's more like dropping out of an elite prep school where everyone has a private tutor, the ornithology club has its own midtown office space, and even Jerry Seinfeld's kids don't make it into the star-studded video yearbook. Like I said in chapter one: You can't spend decades figuring out exactly which machine at the gym makes your ass look buff, how to rush through a crowded grocery store the night before a major holiday, and when to stick a pair of sneakers in your tote bag in case of rain and then—as if none of this matters—casually commit to a place where everyone eats bread and knows what the word *rebar* means.

Take it from "Hope," who followed her husband to the outskirts of Dallas. In Texas, she said, everyone "wore fake eyelashes, had studs on the back pockets of their jeans, and wore ten rings at a time." Over the course of ten years, Hope made great friends. She went out with a bunch of gals once a week and had a "drunk lunch" at a suburban shopping mall Taco Diner. Hope made it there! She did have to set some limits. She broke up with her hairstylist, Rhonda, for example, because her hair "just kept getting blonder." But when her husband found a new job and they moved "up North," she kept feeling like she shouldn't leave her house without makeup. Would they even let her into a restaurant without a manicure? The answer is, ha ha yes. But being coiffed, manicured, and made up was just how Hope rolled back in the big D.

When I left the big NY, I could've used a drunk lunch or two. I haven't had big hair since the eighties—when I used to home perm my bangs—to look like Jo on *The Facts of Life*—but I lugged around other irrational ideas about failure, and superficial definitions of success. For example, I missed being around famous people. In New York City, famous people are everywhere. They usually look a lot less glamorous in person, and much smaller, in every dimension. Well, move to most other places in America, and you will never again see Robert

Downey Jr. strolling inconspicuously out of a Kenneth Cole store. You may *think* you saw Robert Downey Jr. once or twice. Like, at the public library. But it will always turn out to be a foreign man in a weird hat. I've never even seen a Kenneth Cole store in Wisconsin and, by Madison Avenue standards, that brand is the participation ribbon of gay cubicle fashion.

I didn't walk around Wisconsin kvetching about it, of course. I couldn't even say the word *kvetching*, because almost nobody would've understood it. But since leaving the epicenter of Yiddish slang and settling down in the land of feed corn, I can tell you this: Stop asking yourself if you failed. That's the wrong question. Free-floating negative thoughts are not productive. According to Buddhists, in fact, every time we arbitrarily put ourselves down, we break our own hearts just a little bit. Reader, don't break your own heart. That's why God invented teenagers. And Fitbits. And when that heartbreak happens, Robert Downey Jr. may not be around anymore to cheer you up.

HOW HAVE I FAILED?

Rather than asking yourself if you've failed in an arbitrary and open-ended way, pitch yourself a more productive—and provocative—question. Try this curveball: "*How have I failed?*"

I don't want to blow your mind too early in the program. But this here is a self-help book, not a Christmas-cookie exchange. The precise contours of big life decisions only become clear when we face them directly, with cool baseball metaphors. And if there is one thing upon which all experts can agree, it's that everyone must learn how to deal with life's sudden benders.

Everyone has to learn how to fail. That's because failure happens
to everyone. It happens to astronauts, to chess champions, to
Navy SEALs, and sometimes even to Serena Williams.

Listen, Reader, if the word *failure* bums you out a little bit,
I can sympathize. Every time I have that recurring dream
about failing French class—which, according to dream logic,
I somehow forgot to attend—I wake up in a cold sweat. Of
course I do! Everyone knows that if you fail high school French,
you're basically done with life. Nonetheless, experts on failure
say we shouldn't compound our failure by beating ourselves up.
We should try thinking of failure as a learning experience. If a
baseball player strikes out, does he kick the dirt and throw his
bat? Well, anyway. I'm not calling you a failure because you want
to move. I'm just asking, in what very specific ways is your
current location not working out?

For many of us, the most common cause of failure is
money. New York City, for example, attracts so many students,
struggling artists, low-paid dancers, unemployed actors, and
kindhearted social workers that when you put them together
with all the Pilates instructors and public school teachers,
you have a motherfucking truckload of dreamers who just
got dumped into a financial nightmare. Most people cope with
it, however they can. Six years into my graduate program, and
buried in credit card debt along with the rest of America, for
example, I took a staff job with the city. I was hired to do
"change management" in a "human resources software imple-
mentation." I didn't really know what that meant, and I still
don't. Most of the time, I felt like we were being held captive in
a cubicle jail by Accenture consultants. That job was so boring,
I actually fell asleep just now writing about it. But I showed

up almost every day, almost on time. Know why? Because I like eating.

But failure isn't always about cash flow. Not long before she passed away, the great Elaine Stritch moved back to her home state of Michigan. Elaine Stritch was a Tony Award–winning actress, a theatrical celebrity, a precious urban gem. Yet, after a hip replacement, she reportedly found it too difficult to get around in New York. I wasn't surprised. New Yorkers are incredibly good, helpful people. Still, as anyone with a disability (or small children) will tell you, the public transportation system is a shit show. A sizable percentage of the men who ride the subway must suffer from fibromyalgia, because little old ladies and toddlers will be holding on for dear life while these guys man-spread their shit all the way to lower Manhattan like they're Vladimir Putin. If you're lucky, one of them might finish clipping his fingernails onto the floor and give up his seat before you get to South Ferry. Say what you will about Michigan, haters, but it's easier on the hips.

Subway romantic Cari Luna left New York when she failed to stop her neighborhood from gentrifying itself into a tacky suburb. She was especially disappointed when the former home of the poet W. H. Auden was torn down and replaced with a "crappy but expensive bistro." Never mind that most suburbs in America don't even have a crappy bistro and that in New York, crappy means the *pommes-frites* weren't fried in organic duck fat. But if you're a New Yorker, and you are too busy reading poetry to eat substandard fries, a gentrification bistro can truly be the last straw.

For some people, failure arises like a faint whisper of self-awareness. For a long time, the columnist Andrew Sullivan apparently failed to notice that New York was a big city. "Why would anyone want to make it here?" Sullivan woke up one day and asked. "The human beings are stacked on top of one another in vast towers that create dark, narrow caverns in between." What's more, the traffic was perpetually gridlocked and competed with "every conceivable noise and every imaginable variation on the theme of human rage and impatience." Fortunately, Sullivan was able to pack up his suntan lotion and relocate to a friendlier clime. Crisis averted! Because if he had stayed in the city one second longer, he may also have realized that a startling number of pizza places are named Ray's, Original Ray's, or Famous Original Ray's, and suspiciously, very few of them appear to be famous, original, or owned by a person named Ray.

New Yorkers may excel at copy-branding their pizza, but they have no monopoly on failure. Remember "Jamie," with the paranoid pan-slinging grandpa? After several years teaching Latin in the District of Columbia, Jamie decided it was time to return to her hometown. She made this decision haltingly, after a bad breakup. "I wasn't ready to go it alone, severely damaged and depressed, in an unfriendly city," she told me. She liked D.C., especially its diversity of culture. But she also missed the close-knit community in Buffalo; she pined for a smaller place where neighbors "adopted entire families," whether they moved to town with a stockpile of weaponized cookware or not.

For some people, the reasons for failure are obvious and explicit: They carelessly wear down their hips, they crave better *croque-monsieurs*, or they suddenly notice that combustion engines are noisy and skyscrapers are tall. For so many of us, however, the big realization—that we are no longer making it there—doesn't come in a flash of clairvoyance. Our insights are more gradual. Our readiness to leave creeps up like an unexpected case of shingles on a remote part of the body. Okay, it was my tailbone. It was pretty itchy for a long time. Then it went from itchy to burning hot almost overnight, and I couldn't sit down for weeks. Point is, failure doesn't even seem like a real, actionable life problem until . . . something seismically shifts. That's when we've reached:

THE TIPPING POINT

One of these tipping-point people was "Reilly," who bought a country home after living for many years in the hypercompetitive, high-tech Bay Area. She had lifestyle concerns for years before her family moved. Academic pressure was so acute in San Francisco that her kids were staying up until three in the morning studying, and many students were cheating or otherwise buckling under the pressure to get flawless grades. Even after she concluded that she wanted something different for her kids, it took her husband another two years to find the right opportunity.

But Reilly remembers one defining moment—her personal tipping point—when she was sitting at a meeting of her book club, at which "all the girls talked about was how their cleaning ladies didn't fold their laundry right" and other privileged, status-oriented claptrap. "I just sat there," Reilly said, "wanting to stab myself in the neck." Instead of murdering herself, she bought a gentleman's farm in the Midwest. Her new home is a case study in rustic chic and a model of tidy domesticity. But when she's not designing her own menus or landscaping the yard, she drives farm equipment around that estate like a laid-back Eva Gabor.

"Mandy," the pediatrician who lived in Seattle, put up with a lot of doubt and frustration before deciding to quit the Northwest altogether. She fielded snide comments from acquaintances about her lack of exercise. She bore the ever-increasing financial strain of living in a city full of Internet start-ups, i.e. people who paid for new houses in cash. She did her best to tolerate their infernal pescatarianism.

Ultimately, it wasn't mountain climbing or software programmers that pushed her over the edge. It was when she told her colleagues that she was pregnant with her third child. Rather than high-fiving her for her fecundity, bravery, or obviously active sex life (woot), they asked if she had "intended to get pregnant." These people were doctors, for *children*. Superbreeders were their bread and butter! They'd have been psyched if she had left work early to run a marathon, Mandy thought, or taken her dog out on a coffee date. But having a third baby? What kind of buck wild promiscuity was that?

Mandy's story spoke to me in a very personal way. Not because I have a shitload of kids or because I love potlucks. Reader, I hate potlucks. If I want to eat cold food prepared by people I don't know, I go to a sushi bar, where there is also hot wine, waiters, and regular health inspections. Mandy and I did share some deep issues about family life, however. For both of us, having kids was a blessing and a gift which, within the context of city living, also became our biggest failure.

Allow me to give you some background. After fifteen years as a New York resident, I was more than used to failure. I had successes, too, but those moments paled in comparison to my penchant for making bad choices. I'll spare you the details of most of my bad *sexual* choices, since nobody in academia likes to talk about how the male professors sleep with graduate students, but there are still plenty of highlights from my personal failure reel, such as:

- Accruing 10 grand in credit card debt.
- Taking a full-time job while finishing graduate school.
- Not finishing graduate school on time because I had a full-time job.
- Moving five times in three years. By myself.
- Meeting and living with a posh British guy, hoping we'd get married.
- Finding out that guy was ready to get married, for a green card.
- Losing a friend on 9/11.
- 9/11. All of it.

Now, some of those experiences weren't all my fault. I didn't invite those asshole fanatics to attack the city. And it wasn't until that boyfriend banished my schoolbooks and family photographs from the living room—because "nobody" wants to look at personal items or ugly paperbacks—that I fully understood the British upper class and their unfailing standards in living room décor. Karl Marx once wrote that we all make choices within circumstances that aren't in our control. Marx wasn't a huge fan of the British elite, either, and that makes more sense to me now. Because while I moved in with that British guy for love, I *totally* stayed for the Stockholm syndrome.

Just before the second of those five apartment moves, I got injured. It wasn't a drunken street brawl or anything. I was fighting on a martial arts team. I liked it, but mostly I was doing it to avoid writing my dissertation. Then one day, I got my ass kicked and broke the wrist on my dominant arm. My room-mate at the time—a salt-of-the-earth comedian named Jill, and one of the only friends I retained in that Wisconsin breakup—kept promising my arm would heal. But every day, as I wiggled my wrist around in my cast, it felt worse. Finally, one night, I was out drinking at a grunge bar near our apartment in Alphabet City and this random guy next to me gave me some free medical advice.

"Your cast is loose," Random Bar Guy said. "I'm not a doctor or anything, but it looks fucked up."

I believed him that he wasn't a doctor. Since he also wasn't a therapist, I didn't bother to tell him how I got that bad cast in the first place. After waiting in the ER for an hour, because hospitals apparently play favorites with gunshot victims, I got in to see the on-call orthopedic resident. He wasn't 100 percent sure what to do.

"Should I stop the cast at the elbow?" he said, "or go all the way to the shoulder?" I didn't know the right answer. But I did have a yellow belt, and some of my dissertation written. And he looked like a taller version of Harry Shum Jr. So I flirted with him until he gave me the shorter cast.

After the barfly diagnosed me, I followed up again with my school clinic. Turned out, the supervising doctor who had signed off on the handsome baby doctor's cast hadn't really paid attention to what should have been an obvious problem. In fact, the supervising doctor was facing medical malpractice charges. So when I brought the cast to the attention of the clinic manager, she looked like she might get violently ill, then got me an urgent appointment with a fancy Upper East Side doctor, who told me that not only had my arm not been healing for two weeks, it had actually become *more broken*. The only upside of this entire fiasco was that for its duration, I was completely unable to work on my dissertation. Achievement unlocked!

Eight weeks with a cast up to my shoulder and six months of physical therapy later, the arm worked again. During the healing period, whenever Jill had to leave town, she baked me quiches. This was incredibly helpful, except when she forgot to preslice them and I had to eat straight from the center of the pie dish with a fork. We spent a lot of time that year—Jill, her sweet yellow lab, and me—sitting together in the apartment foyer, which we called the "living room." We'd turned the real living room into Jill's bedroom, with a big velvet curtain for quasi privacy. It was a perfect situation for exactly nobody, except for the dog, who lacked opposable thumbs and was pretty psyched she didn't have to deal with any pesky doorknobs.

At least two of us in that apartment were clinically depressed. I worried that I'd never finish school, that I'd be a terminally low-income adjunct teacher, that I'd never fall in love, and that if my arm never healed, I might have to eat the center of quiches for the rest of my godforsaken life. Jill tried to take a longer view.

"You know, Erin," she'd say, sitting two feet across from me, right next to the front door. "Someday, we are going to look back and remember these as the best years of our lives."

"So true," I would say, forcing a laugh and waving my crooked arm. "We'll think back to the years when we were cool hipsters living in Alphabet City."

It sounded convincing at the time. But now, if I'm being perfectly honest, I still remember those years—with the bright neon luster of a grungy bar sign—as being pretty fucking depressing.

At this point in my faux-hipster chronicles, it would be reasonable for you to stop and ask, Why wasn't *that* your tipping point? I was doing a pretty darn good job at failing, so why didn't I accept defeat? Why didn't I move someplace where I could afford to rent more than one room? Why didn't I go finish my dissertation in a town with more licensed doctors and crappy yet affordable bistros? Why didn't I go finish my dissertation anywhere? I was broken, in more ways than one, and 9/11 hadn't even happened yet. OMFG, it was about to get so much worse.

The only answer I can give is that New York had become my home. My life wasn't going anywhere, in a practical sense. But it wasn't technically moving backward, either. I had only myself to keep alive, and I was doing an acceptable job at that. I knew my way around the grocery store, which is not nothing when you're in a hurry. I had a few friends. I had a functional arm. For a while, until I fired him for asking too many hard questions, I even had a good therapist. Most important—as we discussed in the previous chapter—you can love something and hate it at the same time. And I had lived in New York long enough to know that even when life there hit the lowest of the lows, it could still hit the highest of earthly highs.

You put up with the dead poets and the crappy bistros, Reader, because there are so many living poets and great bistros.

My friend Justine and I hung out regularly at the Corner Bistro on West Fourth Street. She lived nearby, on Charles Street, in a studio so small and old she had to wash her dishes in the bathtub. The Corner Bistro was packed, every night, because it had big cheap juicy burgers and the crispiest, saltiest fries. We spent countless Sunday afternoons there, drinking beer and talking about one of five topics: our bad boyfriends, our dead-end jobs, our cramped apartments, our broken bodies, and the truly fabulous hamburgers. Not gonna lie to you: As depressed as I was, I still remember those as some of the best hamburgers of my life.

Balthazar had opened around that time. It was way out of my budget, but it was a fun place. We sought out Balthazar in the dark days after 9/11: me, Justine, her bad boyfriend, and my bad boyfriend. The city was still under military lockdown. The bar was quiet; everyone was still in shock. I waited anxiously for hopeful news about my friend Bob, a firefighter. That news never came. But I still remember that meal, because I hadn't eaten much for days. In a moment of emotional release, I ordered a steak, rare. I gulped it down with a plate of fries and several glasses of red wine. Since cigarettes were still allowed in bars back then, and none of us particularly cared if we lived or died at that moment, we chain-smoked through the entire meal. *Carpe diem, motherfuckers.* It was a terrible time. But if I had ever considered leaving New York before, there was no way I'd leave it now. Not in that condition.

Eventually, sunnier days returned, and Balthazar lasted through those seasons, too. When I finally finished grad school, for example, I asked Tara if she'd take notes at my dissertation defense. My adviser had suggested I find someone to do that so I didn't have to pay attention while we were talking. Or something. "I'd be honored," Tara said. It's possible she misheard the question.

Maybe I should've warned her that the dissertation defense would be like one of those office meetings that could've just been an e-mail thread. But Tara is the epitome of a good sport. Until my brother moved to the city years later, Tara was the closest thing I had to family in New York. At holidays, she invited me out to her childhood home on Long Island. For a while, we were roommates. It was Tara who taught me that there is no better breakfast than coffee and a cigarette. Given how emotionally unstable I was back then, I maybe should've stuck with food. Or at least smoked Marlboro *Lights*. But who knew?

After the defense, we walked from Washington Square Park to Balthazar. We sat at a table in the back, ate oysters, and drank champagne. To be honest, it was one of the proudest days of my life, although once again, it turned out somewhat less optimally for Tara. At lunch, a woman at the next table dropped her spoon into a dish and coated Tara in melted butter. Later, it was a windy night and she was knocked down by a falling awning on her way to my graduation party in the West Village. She went to the hospital with a concussion. Scary stuff, but also a great story. I'm sure she looks back on it as one of the best nights of my life.

All of which brings me to my tipping point. Earlier, I said I stayed in New York because it had become my home and, despite all the failing, the highs balanced out the lows. Eventually, though, that balance tipped. Like Mandy—who tolerated the 26.2 crowd in Seattle right up until they slut-shamed her third pregnancy—the decision that got me to finally step over that line was parenthood.

Look, I know I just poked a wasp's nest. I know that the topic of fertility makes women—on all sides, of every issue—feel angry and defensive. I understand that. I feel angry and defensive every time I hear the word *infertility*. If men are impotent, they call it *erectile dysfunction*, but women with reproductive challenges are called *infertile*? Where's our friendly euphemism? Thanks, patriarchy.

I have to be honest about my experience, though. This is a real-talk manual about moving. It's not about finding happiness by cleaning your closet or eating chicken soup for your soul. And whatever you think about reproduction—or Mandy's decision to have a third child, when so many stray dogs need coffee—parenthood is a game changer. It turns your life upside down. You want the babies, and you love the babies. But babies are a buttload of responsibility, and parenting is motherfucking hard. It's harder than spending eight years in graduate school. It's definitely harder than getting your arm broken, or more broken, inside the wrong cast. It might even be harder than getting crushed by an awning or breaking your face. Hmm, I should ask Tara about that sometime.

Despite what you may think when you're single and in grad school, babies don't necessarily want to sit in a booth at a bistro while you drink red wine, eat raw meat, and chain-smoke your life away. They require slightly more attention than you are accustomed to providing your friend on a rainy Sunday at the Corner Bistro. You can swap depression narratives with a girl-friend over a perfectly grilled hamburger—and feel like this is very, very difficult—right up until you try to breastfeed a fussy baby on a stalled subway car while the man sitting next

to you loud-talks on the phone to his wiener doctor about his
impotence.

Our baby started with a blind date. Just eight short years after
starting grad school, and a month before I moved a sixth time,
my friend Cheryl said she knew a guy. "I think his name is
Mike," she said. She was right. Mike was a friend of Mark. Mark
was married to Jenni. Jenni was friends with Cheryl. I knew
Cheryl from college. In the context of this group of friends—
all of whom were Jewish—Mike and I were like two single
Catholics wandering down the same aisle at a kosher grocery
store. A few weeks later, he called me at work. He asked me to
choose a place, and because I (always) lived downtown, I chose
the Art Bar, a cozy spot just up from the Corner Bistro.

"Great!" he said. He sounded boyish and sincere, and I liked
that because New York usually crushes that like a water bug.
"Just so we can recognize each other, I have brown curly hair
and glasses, and I'll be wearing a lime green shirt."

"A LIME GREEN SHIRT?!" yelled my co-worker Luke
over the partition when I recounted the phone call. "Did he
actually *say* that?" Luke, who always came to cubicle jail impec-
cably dressed, thought "lime green" sounded ugly. I took his
concern under advisement, but went on the date anyway.

Turned out, the shirt was more of a light green. It's not super
germane to the story, but I wanted you to have that visual. And
he was cute: tall, with droopy hazel eyes like a puppy dog's. I
discovered this twenty minutes after we'd agreed to meet,
because he was late, which should've been a red flag for me. Since
he was late, I started drinking without him, which should've
been a red flag for Mike. After a few glasses of Sancerre, we

decided to have dinner at a seafood restaurant on Jane Street. During the meal, Mike drew a map of the world on the paper tablecloth, and I spilled melted butter down the front of my shirt. And that pretty much sums up our entire relationship.

Mike and I dated for about a year before I got a teaching job and moved to Rhode Island. Despite that—and the fact that one morning, he woke up and saw me eating a Milk Dud that I had slept on all night—we ended up getting married and starting a family. Those things didn't necessarily happen in that order, however. The Milk Dud thing happened before the baby. The baby happened just a wee bit before the marriage. For the record, Reader, the conventional order of things is probably easier. Still, half of all pregnancies in this country are unscheduled. When life doesn't give you a sleeveless shirt, sometimes you gotta tear the sleeves off yourself, know what I'm saying? Besides, I couldn't blame myself. It was my sister's fault.

At the end of my first semester as a bona fide professor, my sister came out to visit. I showed her around my office, she stayed overnight in my dumpy apartment, then we drove down to see Mike in New York. About twenty minutes into the trip, I realized that I had forgotten my birth control.

"When did your last cycle end?" she asked. Caroline was training to be a doctor, which helps to explain why she would ask such a technical question.

"It *just* ended," I told her. I was about 37 percent sure that was true.

"Well," she said, "a lot of women your age try to get pregnant for several months, with no luck. It's pretty unlikely." I think that's what she said, anyway. I wasn't really paying attention.

When Mike and I got together, I reported the straight facts: Caroline said there was almost no chance of pregnancy. He was fine with it because Caroline was basically a doctor. I was fine with it because we had already talked about getting married one time in Miami for a minute. And in all seriousness, we both wanted to be parents anyway. About twenty-two days later—after several holiday parties, some class-D anxiety medication, and at least one soak in a scalding hot Jacuzzi—I realized I was pregnant. I called the doctor.

"Caroline!" I yelled into the phone like a crazed pregnant woman who had suddenly stopped taking her anxiety medication. "Remember when you told me there was no way I'd get pregnant?!"

Audible gasp. Caroline knew I was about to blame her. Of course she did. The whole point of younger sisters is to be the object of blame when things don't go well, so you feel better about your own bad choices. You might not even have made those bad choices if *they* hadn't stolen your thunder in the first place! So blaming them is completely fair and works out for everyone, the end.

"You gave me the wrong information!" she screamed back. But I could hear her smiling. I was smiling too. "Oh my God!" she said. "Congratulations!"

Over the next week, Mike and I picked up where we had left that Miami conversation, which was somewhere between "probably" and "eventually." We wanted this baby, real bad. We thought of the pregnancy as a miracle; the best thing that could possibly have happened. So we shotgunned the nuptials. Somehow—despite living in two different cities and having two demanding jobs—we found time to make my mom plan a wedding.

The baby, like her dad, was late. She was a glorious and demanding creature. I left my job and moved back to New York, where I took her to music and dance classes and cultivated her social network so she was surrounded by a wide diversity of wealthy people. I strolled her around Central Park and fantasized about how she would grow up to be one of those sophisticated New Yorkers, like Lin-Manuel Miranda or Scarlett Johansson, never to be sullied by suburban strip malls or opioids. Before she was ten, she'd know the secret New York name for a giant cockroach. Before the age of fifteen, she'd know exactly what shoes to wear while walking through the rat-infested garbage on Fourteenth Street. Spoiler: The best answer is never flip-flops.

Motherhood was a tough transition for me, but not because we were under financial strain. All those years, while I had been going into debt, Mike had been saving money. Mike worked sixty to eighty hours a week at a law firm, and his undying devotion to work was handsomely rewarded. I definitely didn't have the same financial burdens as "Hillary," for example, who left Los Angeles not simply because of smog and overpopulation and drought, but because her wife lost her job and the school system refused to mainstream their special-needs child. Before leaving L.A., she told me, she went from feeling "frustrated" to feeling "disgusted and discouraged." She missed L.A.'s superior tacos, but not enough to give up the national health care in New Zealand.

It was just that, for me, everything became exponentially more complicated. My mom had to sleep on the couch when she visited, for weeks at a time. When my dad came, they had to pay for a hotel. We needed a bigger apartment, but that kind of financial commitment meant Mike would truly never be there, and he already almost never left the office. Small matters of urban living disheartened me, too. A few sketchy encounters in the park forced me to restrict my Central Park meandering to the main thoroughfares. Had city life always been this raw and rough, I wondered, and I just never noticed? Then one day a pit bull ran up and peed all over a dead bird, and I had my answer.

If you're ambivalent about the place you live, a baby will intensify that uncertainty. Resilient people—of which I am not one—can adapt. By the time our second baby arrived, we still hadn't found a bigger apartment, or even decided whether to move. We did the New York thing of waiting for a neighbor to move out so we could knock down a wall, but then—when he finally did—we couldn't commit to the cost. School district variation and overcrowding made every decision about where to live fraught and—for us—therefore paralyzing. So we stayed put. Our superintendent, Alfredo, helped me set up a third bedroom. Which was actually our second bathroom. To make room for a crib (and only a crib), Alfredo had to remove the sink, the shower stalls, *and* the toilet. That, I'm told, is called living the dream.

It didn't help that we literally lost the kids.

Twice.

The first time was at the Barnes and Noble store on Broadway. My older daughter wandered off into the children's book section as I paged through some cookbooks. I didn't pay attention because, frankly, I thought she was just toddling over to the reading carpet to listen to some other kid's nanny. But in a flash, she was gone. After looking upstairs for a few minutes, I grew frantic. I panicked and bolted to the escalator.

"I can't find my daughter!" I screeched at the security guard.

Just as I started bounding down the up escalator toward the exit door—scanning for the child predator I was certain had snatched my kid—I heard her. She'd gotten stuck behind a tall stack of books and couldn't find her way back. When I picked her up, all I could think was, *What would I have told Mike?* The brain generates strange questions when it's high on terror adrenaline. My immediate next thought was, *Holy fuck,* that security guard did not blink an *eyelash* while I screamed at her face. Make no mistake, city moms: Those guards are *not* there to save your children from predators. They are there to save the books.

The second time we lost them, it was Easter. We went down to Riverside Park to participate in a free neighborhood egg hunt with our friends Jimmy and Michelle. It was a beautiful New York spring day and, as we discovered, a very popular event. The organizers divided the crowd into age groups to control the flow, but when they blew the whistle, the kids disappeared underneath a stampede of about five thousand people—none of whom were remotely religious, but all of whom were hell-bent on getting some motherfucking eggs. We found them after several minutes, before the next stampede started. But only because I started screaming again, and Mike is the size of a mature evergreen tree.

I tried to find equilibrium as a parent in the city, but every new challenge knocked me off balance again. Just before our second daughter was born, for example, daughter number one was caught up in a fire drill. For some reason—her hyperaware personality or her hyperclueless babysitter—she got traumatized by the sound. After that, she was afraid of the smoke detectors in our apartment. She was afraid to ride in the elevator because it sometimes got stuck and set off a clanging alarm. At night, Mike took to sleeping on the floor next to her, holding her hand through the slats of her crib.

To self-help myself through this crisis, I read every parenting website and book I could find. Nothing helped because parenting websites are 90 percent about sleep training and 10 percent about BPA poisoning. Then one day, my daughter saw a video about a kid pretending to be a circus strongman and decided to become one herself. Her name was—and I think you'll agree it was very creative—Strongman. She would pace around her bedroom several times a day, talking about her life in the circus and flexing her muscles for dramatic effect. Looking back, it was kind of hilarious. And eventually, this imaginary persona helped her get past her fears. But it went on for months. And, Reader, let me say this one thing: When your toddler stops functioning normally and stops answering to her given name—and starts referring to herself in the third person as a circus freak—it's not obvious that shit's gonna work itself out.

But the ultimate tipping factor—the horrible Medusa that finally turned my uncertain heart to stone—was kindergarten. I'm not going to try to wealthsplain this. Or whitesplain it. Or Manhattansplain it, if that's even a thing, but it definitely should be. We didn't love the public school in our neighborhood. We wanted our kids to get a great education, and we could afford private school. That was our choice, and our frame of reference, and I'm not asking for sympathy. All I ask is that you keep an open mind, because I'm about to make fun of rich people.

Finding a private school in New York City is exactly like an Easter egg hunt. Except instead of five thousand ambitious, competitive, high-strung people trampling your children to death in order to get their hands on a plastic egg with a stale Hershey's kiss inside, there are fifty thousand people with sharp elbows trying to get their kids into Harvard fourteen years early. Wealthy elites in Manhattan can be very nice people. But get in their way on a kindergarten tour and they will stab you in the neck with a jumbo crayon and stuff your bloody cadaver into the painting smock cabinet without ever looking back.

In many towns throughout the country, like the ones where Mike and I grew up, sending a child to kindergarten is a tender, heartwarming rite of passage. In New York, it was a little bit more like soul murder. During one private school tour, we sat down in the auditorium of an Anglican school with some friends—and hundreds of other parents who were also trying to look spiritual—and listened to the headmaster joke that their annual tuition was the "financial equivalent of buying a brand-new BMW every year and driving it into the Hudson River." We all laughed. I feel certain that Gandhi would've wanted it that way.

The process for applying to private school has been exhaustively examined, and mocked, in a lot of magazines and newspapers. In case you haven't been lucky enough to read those pity pages, here's a summary:

1. Call five to ten schools, a year in advance, for materials.
2. As the application dates approach, line up babysitters and leave work early/go in late, so you and your spouse can attend school tours. Suck up to the headmaster, if you have something witty to say. If not, hide in the back and STFU.

3. Generate a list of people whose parents or grandparents or great-great-grandparents may have gone to one of the desired schools and whose family might recommend you.

4. Even if they don't recommend you, if they are famous, name drop them into a conversation anyway.

5. Fill out all personal statements about your child's academic strengths and weaknesses, list names of Ivy League colleges one or both parents attended, and indicate how much money you definitely plan to donate to those colleges every year.

6. Find the cutest pictures of your child ever taken. Your four-year-old's picture should convey confidence, self-possession, maturity, intelligence, and family wealth. Be tasteful but remember that the trustafarians will hire a professional photographer to pose their twins in front of an easily recognizable landmark, such as the Great Barrier Reef, the Eiffel Tower, or their own Fifth Avenue penthouse apartment.

7. Personally deliver all applications, with application fees of up to a thousand dollars per school. Do not entrust this responsibility to postal people, who can't possibly understand the importance of these materials. For the same reason, also don't entrust it to your husband.

8. After a reasonable amount of time, but not a desperate one, call to schedule an appointment for the "playdate."

9. Before the "playdate," which is basically a job interview, drill your kid on math facts and vocabulary. Remind your child not to cry, whine, suck on fingers, lose focus, push, sass, interrupt, or get any answers wrong. You can

bribe her with the promise of material rewards, but let her know that if she mentions the bribe in public, the offer will be retracted like lightning.

10. If she gets in, start figuring out how you're going to pay forty thousand a year per child for the next twelve years, plus fees and donations, while also saving for college.

11. But don't worry, she probably won't.

Gross, right? But we did it. We did all of it. We did the interviews. The fake playdates. The "intelligence" testing. The sucking up to headmasters who made obscene jokes about obscene wealth. We worried through all of it, because we didn't have inherited savings, or a summer home, or legacy status. We had one high-paying career between us. But we also had no time for a relationship, and supporting a private school education for two kids would mean running even faster on that gerbil wheel. In the end, our daughter got into exactly one school, where a friend of ours put in a good word. And we loved it. They had the messiest art room in the world, a rooftop playground, and mandatory large block building time. But there was no elementary school program. Our daughter could stay for two years; after that, we'd have to do it all again.

One day, I was standing outside our building, chatting with Dio, our grandfatherly doorman. Dio was an actual grandfather, as well as the closest thing our kids had to a grandfather for several thousand miles. One of my neighbors put her kids (and their nanny) in a limo and sent them off to their beach house. As she waved good-bye to Jeeves, she told me her daughter had just gotten into Brearley, an elite all-girls school that goes

from kindergarten all the way through high school. Then she
got in a cab and drove away. *That's it*, I thought. *I'm leaving.*

All of my agita was bouncing around, high and dry, in this
atmosphere of megaprivilege. It was a bitch, girl, and if we'd had
no choice about where to send our kids, we'd have sent them
to public school and made it work. But since we had means,
schooling became a massive BPA-free Tupperware container for
so many other issues—our work/life balance or lack of it, our
marital equality or lack of it, our community or lack of it. It was
like having status anxiety, in both directions! We didn't want to
miss out on great opportunities in New York, but because Mike
and I had both transplanted from smaller towns—where we had
gone to both public and parochial schools—the issue of schooling
also made us feel out of place. We had made it there . . . but
had we?

Several of my friends left New York right around this time.
One woman, let's call her "Carolyn," had twin boys. After epic
fertility interventions, they bought an apartment right next to
a public school. When the twins turned five, that school was
deemed overcrowded. The district held a lottery, which they
lost. Carolyn decided to apply to a church-affiliated private
school instead, and they loved it. Success! For two years, anyway,
until that school rejected their third son. Sorry, no space! At
which point, they moved to suburban Connecticut, where the
local public school could accommodate *all* of their kids, at the
same goddamn time.

I feel like parenthood is one of those phases in life—like
your first year out of college or the putrid entirety of seventh
grade—that grabs you by the neck and chokes you until you
gasp for breath. If you don't relate to this choking metaphor and

you have raised kids, you are obviously a better parent than I am. But for me, getting free of that chokehold forced a reevaluation of my priorities. Parenthood turns some people into marathon runners. It makes some people fatter. It convinces other people to divorce their spouses and become yoga instructors. I don't know why that is. But they're always white women, it's always yoga, and I *never* see it coming.

By the most superficial elite standards of Manhattan, I was still making it. I got regular pedicures and occasional blowouts. I could spot a fashion model on a crowded sidewalk based solely on the puffiness of her overcoat and the puppylike hugeness of her feet. One time, Mike and I got invited to a movie premiere, and at the reception afterward, we danced next to Jennifer Lopez. Neither of us could take our eyes off her. We still lived in a gorgeous neighborhood way uptown, had a diverse crowd of friends, and enjoyed some of the best shows and restaurants in the world, except Per Se, because c'mon, nobody is that privileged.

But parenthood challenged my definition of success. Every time we tried to hire a babysitter and go out to dinner, one of the kids got sick and threw up. I wanted them to grow up near amazing museums, but not if they never saw their dad at dinnertime. Or bedtime. I wanted them to go to public school, but not if they had to send their backpacks through a metal detector every morning. I wanted to raise them in our cool art deco building, close to Harlem and Columbia University, but not if it meant our second kid had to sleep in a moldy bathroom with one tiny window that looked out onto an air shaft coated in pigeon shit. The lows and the highs were out of whack. The balance was bust.

Reader, have you reached your tipping point? If you still aren't sure, let's review some tough questions. Does your job feel like cubicle jail? Do your hips hurt? Do your co-workers love your dog but hate your children? Why can't those basic bitches in your book club fold their own damn laundry? Also, why the chicken-fried fuck would you joke about school tuition being so high that it's like driving a car into a river? That's insane.

Well, I didn't know for sure that moving would fix anything. But after fifteen years of running on that gerbil wheel, we decided to jump off.

Chapter 3

NOBODY LEAVES WITHOUT
A FIGHT

MAKING IT HAPPEN

Some things in life are easier said than done. Some things aren't even that easy to say. I don't even bother trying to pronounce *Worcestershire* anymore; I just say steak sauce. Similarly, it may be hard for some of you to *discuss* moving, let alone to make it happen.

If you've gotten as far as this chapter, though, you've already come a long way! Maybe you've acknowledged some failure. Maybe you've mentioned to a friend that you're contemplating a change. Maybe you've had extensive discussions with your spouse—both at couples therapy and on the sidewalk afterward—and you've accepted that neither the bookstore security guard nor the admissions staff at Brearley is ever going to save your children.

If that skinny bundle of deliberations describes your life right now, you're in good company. According to *USA Today*, which looks like fake news but is actually just fast news, the peak ages for urban living are twenty-five to twenty-seven years old. That's because young adults often experiment with identities and lifestyles before they settle down and/or start families. Some kids graduate from college, flock to big cities, and live large on bank salaries. Some of them move back in with their parents, because even Cleveland is expensive when you're unemployed. By the age of forty-one, though, an estimated one fifth of those capering city kids has moved out to the suburbs. That might not seem like a lot, but as mathematicians know, small fractions of big numbers are still pretty big. That's why casinos sometimes let people win. That's also why, even when you have an uncommon Chinese surname that is literally one in a million, there are still *a thousand* other people like you.

According to an Empire Center for Public Policy study, more than one million people migrate out of New York City every decade. One recent *New York Times* piece suggested that if you break down the out-migration numbers by race, young African Americans are moving out of the city at some of the highest rates—because of racism, the appeal of bigger black communities, and better financial opportunities in smaller cities.

If you live in a big city and haven't landed a high-paying job—or reached the age of maturity on your trust fund—a duplex in Houston might be looking pretty good right about now. Maybe you've even tested out the idea of leaving with a few small gestures: You signed up for a cooking class in anticipation of having a real kitchen. You asked your neighbor to water your dead houseplants while you visit an old friend in New Orleans. You called your agent and asked him to start booking voice-overs, because you're not sure that *High Maintenance* ever films on location in western Ohio.

Ideally, your plans will just materialize. When "Ruby's" husband first got the phone call about a job opportunity in Scottsdale, which came out of nowhere, they laughed. They'd given zero thought to leaving New York. They said no on three separate occasions before they decided it was madness to turn down an opportunity for advancement that his New York job would probably never present. So they turned their failure into a life experiment. "If it didn't work," Ruby said, "we'd move back." They totally expected that it wouldn't work.

But not everyone gets a recruitment phone call. Sometimes they just have inklings of self-doubt. When "Hallie" and her husband had their first baby, they were both gainfully employed as doctors in Boston. They wanted to move closer to grand-parents. But Hallie was from California and "Nate" was from Wisconsin, and although they deliberated the pros and cons of each location, they couldn't close the deal. So they did the next best thing to careful deliberation, which was to flip a coin. They did a few practice runs first, to see how it would feel. When Nate flipped the coin for real and the coin came up for Wisconsin, Hallie called two out of three. He still won.

Gambling is a perfectly acceptable way to make important life decisions, as long as everyone accepts the outcome (or the second outcome). If you'd be equally happy living in an expensive city on the Eastern Seaboard, a far-flung suburb of Atlanta, and a midwestern town where 50 percent of all restaurants are sports bars and the rest have sports playing on TV all the time, then by all means, give that coin a toss. Play a game of bid whist, or a single-elimination speed round of Old Maid. The last or lowest card gets the in-laws!

If you're not okay with leaving a big life decision to a game of chance, I can't say I blame you. You live in a multicultural city where *cornholing* doesn't mean a superfun backyard beanbag game. Now you're going to flip a coin and move to a white-bread suburb where the beanbag definition of *cornholing* is the only one they know? If you need to mull this over some more, then let's play another fun game. It's called:

WELCOME TO YOUR IDENTITY CRISIS!

The natural corollary to the question "Where should I go?" is "Who the fuck am I?" My own crisis of identity started when I was in prison. Let me say a bit more about that.

After I had my first daughter, went back to teaching part-time, and got pregnant with my second, one of my adjunct positions was in a correctional facility in upstate New York. I did it because colleagues had told me it was very rewarding work. And they were right. Besides, what pregnant woman doesn't want to drive two hours upstate to teach in a maximum security men's prison?

One day a week, I left the kid with my younger brother, Anthony. Anthony was finishing an advanced degree in art and had some spare time, so I hired him to work as my manny. He wasn't a professional manny—which is evidently now an actual thing—but he was a fun, loving, cool uncle. Some days, I'd come home to find him and my daughter chatting quietly while they dined on "yo-sauce," their nickname for yogurt and apple-sauce. Other days, I'd come home to find my daughter running around the apartment with her entire stuffed animal collection masking-taped to her body. Like I said, he wasn't a professional. On the other hand, he never let her die. Not once.

One day, up at the prison, I told my senior thesis student about our momentous decision.

"Bill, I'm not sure I'll be able to come to your graduation ceremony. We're leaving New York."

Bill had been a New Yorker his whole life, some of which he'd spent in Brooklyn and the rest of which he'd spent in that building. He asked where we were going.

"Not really sure yet," I said. "We just started formulating a plan. Maybe California or Colorado or Wisconsin."

"Wisconsin?" he chortled. "People don't move *to* Wisconsin."

Let me tell you, Reader, nothing inspires confidence in your geographic prospects like being mocked inside the slammer. But even without the satire, the identity crisis was inevitable. Just as kids amplify your feelings of uncertainty, looking for a new home can amplify self-doubt. Let's say you lived in Los Angeles through your hipster twenties. You just invented a truck that serves gourmet tacos, and you were about to park it in front of a county museum and sell lunch from a big side window, when you discovered that "food trucks" already existed. So you decided to take your invention and move someplace where the local dining scene boils down to a choice between White Castle and Hardee's. You never dreamed of living in rural Missouri. And, as soon as you decide, you feel a rising tide of panic about this alleged life hack. Where *exactly* in that red state will you be living? Is ethnic food legal in that town? Wait, did they just vote to take away their own health care?

Try not to panic. If small-town Missouri doesn't work out, you don't necessarily have to die there. You can drive that taco truck right back to L.A., where you practically invented it. Your ego may get bruised further when you discover that the moment you left, you were stone-cold dead to everyone you used to know. They forgot you like, the microsecond you rolled out with that U-Haul. *See ya, taco girl! Can't wait to see your new house, on Instagram! Good luck finding an affordable ob-gyn!*

Deciding to move can really stir up your inner demons. Just ask "Cara," a woman from Melbourne, Australia, who moved several times around the Eastern Seaboard of the United States before finally settling in Los Angeles for her then-husband's job. Cara told me that for her, the hardest part of moving was right before she went. "It's a terrible limbo," she said, from "the moment when you let slip that you are thinking of moving and you see the hurt on peoples' faces, because you aren't just leaving a place, you are leaving them." Even before you leave, people start to unconsciously write you off. "They find other people to exercise with in the morning or join a new book club or make plans without you," said Cara, and it "makes the waiting to leave so much harder and more miserable."

I don't know Cara personally. I connected with her via the Internet. If we were IRL friends, I'd let her know that nobody exercises in the morning. Those hours are for sitting on the couch nibbling donuts. But it is normal to freak out about your life when you're on the verge of making a change, especially if you're a neurotic person to begin with. I can't even make a menu selection without systematically rejecting every single other option. I don't want just any dinner, I want the *best* dinner. I want *the one* dinner. And before I actually order, I will invariably scream at the waiter: "WAIT, CAN YOU DESCRIBE ALL THE APPETIZER SPECIALS AGAIN??!" If you're like me and every date night is a reenactment of *The Matrix*, then you will need some strategies for coping with your internal turmoil.

BE GRATEFUL!

In times of extreme cases of feeling sorry for ourselves, we are often counseled to focus on the positive. Many self-help gurus promote having a good attitude and believe that motivational nuggets like "Optimism is a choice" and "Success is a state of mind" can help you turn your frown upside down.

Some people will swear, in fact, that just *smiling* can make you feel more positive. If you walk around New York smiling—and you're not holding a bag of money or a Grammy Award—people will think you're either crazy or a pervert. But my mom, who's a psychologist, also condoned this Jedi mind trick.

"So you're saying you're supposed to just walk around smiling for no reason," I asked her, "even if you actually feel like *shit?*"

"I didn't say 'shit.'" (I should have seen that coming. My mom was raised by nuns and still holds Bart Simpson responsible for the decline of civilization.) "But yes," she said, "clinically speaking, smiling can lift your spirits."

If smiling lifts your spirits, Reader, do that! Walk around town with a shit-eating grin on your face *all day* if you want. Go get it, gurrl But personally, I think that's a short-term solution for a long-term problem.

Which brings me to gratitude journals.

It sounds like something one of my mom's iced tea friends made up. But I think it's actually Oprah's fault. Years ago, when Oprah was still the president, she sent her scientists to Papua

New Guinea, where they found that primitive people—unlike us, the highly evolved people who watch daytime TV—*never* get depressed. Like, not ever. Turns out, the primitive people of Papua New Guinea don't have to walk around smiling all day in order to feel happy, because they don't *expect* to feel happy in the first place. They're just so grateful for what they have.

The idea of a gratitude journal is that you channel this primitive instinct and write down happy stuff to keep the shitty stuff in perspective. I will say this: When you're feeling panicked about leaving the place where you found yourself for someplace else where you might lose yourself, you do need some damn perspective. Hashtag: #NotARefugee.

Also, primitive societies truly have taught us a lot of useful shit. We got yoga from the ancient Indians. Baby wearing, which derives from many global cultures, is a perfect solution in modern society. It was definitely part of my parenting approach. Not only was it good for my kids' emotional health to be tethered to my body, but it was also literally the only way I could keep myself from losing them.

Primitive cultures also gave us breastfeeding. When I had my first infant, I joined a breastfeeding collective. Once a week, I'd stroll up to a café on 110th Street, where a bunch of highly educated women would talk about feminism and motherhood while breastfeeding in public. Sometimes I even shopped at the Upper Breast Side, a store which—because of its horrible name alone—may well have scared a generation of women away from the cause of feminism altogether.

Still, is it reasonable to expect that New Yorkers can achieve the positive psychological outlook of Papua New Guineans? Before you answer that, I need to file three objections.

1) America, and even New York, is not a primitive society.

According to scientists, the primitive people of Papua New Guinea are perfectly happy without big cities, prep schools, world-class restaurants, high salaries, and vacation homes. If they could live without these things, why couldn't I just STFU? One answer, I think, is that the primitive people of Papua New Guinea also don't have cities. Or vacations. Or in some cases, homes. I'm not insensitive to their plight. I think *primitive* is an outdated word and I'm intentionally overusing it to be ironic. But real talk, Reader of the Developed World: Isn't it easier to lower your expectations when you have comparatively little vertical distance to cover in the first place?

For most of the years I lived in New York, I had no discretionary income. I ate tuna fish sandwiches from the deli almost every day and went out for a nice meal every six months when my parents visited. But even in that water-bug-infested micro-tenement, I had a roof over my head and lived in close proximity to some uber-fancy people. Anthony and I met Wynton Marsalis one night at the Blue Note. Mike and I once went out on a double date with Tara and her husband and sat at a table right next to Ralph Lauren. He was dining with his lapdog, who (ironically) had her own chair. While seeing a Shakespeare play one night in Central Park, Dick Cavett actually wiped my sweaty forehead with his handkerchief and quipped that "in some cultures, we were now married." He was joking but I never washed my face again.

I went to a Madonna concert once. After making the audience wait for three hours, she then goaded us to buy her swag because her kids "needed a lot of shoes." I have no beef with

Madonna. Madonna is a beast and a badass. But she's also a fully loaded diva. Would the primitive people of Papua New Guinea be disappointed if they couldn't buy one of her shirts? Maybe so. Based on the photos I've seen of Papua New Guinean men standing around in penis sheaths, however, I don't think they spend too much time worrying about what pop star is on their t-shirts, let alone how many pairs of shoes those children need.

2) I'm already grateful for little things. It's the big things that haunt me.

I will stipulate that for some people, positive psychology works. People who live each day to its fullest and give thanks for the little things should do their groove thing. That still doesn't convince me, however, that my little things matter. I mean, I love little things. I love salty pistachios. I love red hots, especially when they're called cinnamon imperials. I love those tiny jumping spiders that my cats chase to death. I love doing yoga. I love cuddling my kids, even though they frequently tell me I have stinky breath as I'm holding them in a loving embrace.

I love taking a steamy hot shower every day and scrubbing my back with a loofah. I don't like that my husband used my loofah on his feet for several months without telling me. On the other hand, I'm so crazy about my orange tabby cat that I sometimes try to make out with him. I love everything about Lin-Manuel Miranda, and his mom, and his Twitter feed. And even though I have a stone-cold heart in the face of Madonna's shoeless children, my heart melts to liquid goo every time I watch a bunch of preschoolers with plastic bats try to make contact with a piñata.

The year we decided to leave, I still loved these little things. It wasn't like I stopped scrubbing my back with a loofah just because I was having an identity crisis and panic attacks. C'mon. I stopped using it because my husband scrubbed his gross man feet all over it.

But let me hit you with this, Dr. Phil: Even if I had meditated every morning on the spiritual magnitude of my loofah, this still would have been the conversation in my head at three A.M.:

Holy shit. I am leaving the city where I have lived for fifteen years. Mike doesn't have a job yet. We could move to California, but what about migrating sharks? I'm leaving almost all my friends, which is like three people, and it took me twenty years to convince them to like me. What about earthquakes? Do you put your head in between your knees or drop and roll or run outside? Also, we have great health insurance right now, and hospitals. And what about urban coyotes! I finally have a job again, and I have to quit. Now I also have to pee. Fuck. Global. Warming.

Newsflash: My insomnia feeds on worries. You don't wake in the middle of the night to think about how much you love your loofah. You wake up to think about how it might feel to be attacked by a coyote, with no colleagues to call, no friends to help, no medical insurance to pay for your wounds, and climate change screwing everything up because really, what do you think drove the fucking coyote into your backyard in the first place?!

Nothing against President Oprah or my mom, but it's just not a fair fight. If you imagine this positive-attitude-during-an-identity-crisis thing like a Venn diagram—two overlapping circles, one labeled BIG PROBLEMS TO SOLVE and one labeled SMALL WAYS TO FEEL BETTER—there isn't too much space in the middle, where the small things actually solve the big problems. You can't stop a coyote attack, even an imagined one, with a loofah.

3) Fuck positivity.

Believe it or not, positive people sometimes find me annoying. I admit that despite the fact that there are some positive people I truly adore. I love Kelly Ripa because she's peppyAF. I adore Ellen DeGeneres and officially nominate her to be the life coach for the entire human race. I've made my feelings about Lin-Manuel Miranda embarrassingly clear. But when an acquaintance buoyantly suggests that I refocus on gratitude, I just want to ask them, "Exactly what is it about *my* problem that makes *you* so uncomfortable?"

I mean really, positive people. Do you think world poverty can be solved through random acts of kindness? When was the last time you cured someone's colon cancer with your homemade banana bread? Have you seen the statistics on global warming lately? *What the fuck are you smiling about?* You want me to keep a gratitude journal? What a coincidence. Because *I* want *you* to shut the fuck up.

My husband has long maintained that my personality is a three-way tie between Larry David, Lewis Black, and Don Rickles. Nobody knows how an Irish Catholic girl raised in the Midwest grew up to have the aggregated personality of three angry Jewish men. According to my DNA study, I'm only 6 percent Jewish, but science can't explain everything, and no matter what the genes say, I'm 100 percent zero fucks.

So anyway, I skipped the gratitude journal. Fell back on my time-tested methods of relieving stress, which are whiskey, Mexican food, and ranting. But while you're doing that, you'll have to proceed with logistics. Sometimes the best way to deal with an identity crisis is just to start moving forward and see if it gets lost behind a tall bookshelf.

STARTER STRATEGY: MAKE A LIST!

Lists are the real deal. They can't clean your closet for you or solve climate change, but lists are the undisputed gold standard of ways to handle logistics that feel overwhelming. Whether you are choosing gifts for the holidays, topics for term papers, picks for your fantasy football teams, clothes for a weekend getaway with your nurse, or qualities you need in a divorce lawyer, a big fat list can sharpen your focus. *Everything* looks more organized, compartmentalized, and manageable in a list.

- Organized
- Compartmentalized
- Manageable

See?

You may recall that my friend Tara took notes for me at my dissertation defense. Not long after that, I spent an entire day reading through her notes and consolidating them into a giant

to-do list of 116 items. Over the next five years, I completed
exactly four of them. So that wasn't a lot. But without the list, I
might have done even less! And when you are moving, every little
speck of organization helps. You can't approach this momentous decision like a clueless teenager who suddenly decides to go
away for college but hasn't applied anywhere, done any on-campus
visits, or even saved the recruitment mailings from that technical
college you've never heard of in Ohio.

Mike and I made sure that list-making was our first stop on
the How to Leave tour. We wrote down a list of criteria that
each of us might want in a new home, then resolved to put the
lists together, cross-reference our priorities, and turn that exercise into a declaration of common goals. We would resolve any
potential conflicts by—oh, you know—*crossing stuff off.*

As the list train pulled into the station, I was feeling *good.* I
might not be a positive person, but I am an obsessive-compulsive
one. Just going through the motions of making a list helps me
tame some of my free-floating crazy. We both showed up to the
cross-reference party, lists in hand.

Mike's list looked something like this:

- Interesting job
- Good salary and benefits
- Close to family
- Near an ocean and mountains

My list looked something like this:

- Good public schools
- Nice community

- Close to family
- Near a big city

There may have been some other criteria, too, but I can't remember and I threw the papers away. That's another thing about which I am compulsive: I view every piece of paper (and art project) that comes into my house as pre-garbage. And these lists weren't exactly fun keepsakes. As it turns out, list making is an effective strategy for identifying common goals *only if you actually have them.* We had the one: living closer to family. But whose family? Because *that's* an easy one to solve.

We shouldn't have been surprised at this outcome. I grew up in a small college town in the Midwest and Mike grew up in Sacramento, which is often called "the Midwest of California." Yet the only decision Mike and I had ever made together was to stay in New York. We had settled the work/life balance question by splitting it down the middle. He did the work. I did the life. Neither of us had envisioned what living together outside of New York would be like. So rather than resolving our questions, the list just raised new ones. It was sort of like when my broken arm got more broken, except in this case, there was no barfly to tell me what to do.

Other than our desire for family togetherness and free child-care from grandparents, list making made it painfully obvious that someone would end up making a sacrifice. Know why, Reader? I'll tell you, and I'm going to pull out my boss lady voice so you know I'm serious. Because small towns with a great community; interesting, high-paying jobs; abundant scenic oceanfront housing; award-winning public schools that are near Grandma's house; and great gay nightclubs *don't fucking exist in this country.*

RELIABLE STRATEGY: CHOOSE SEATTLE!

Nobody in America considers moving without, at some point, looking at Seattle. I get that. Seattle has a lot going for it. Mountains. Ocean. Salmon. A pretty laid-back, educated populace and (compared to New York, anyway) shorter commutes. Does Seattle have sunshine? No. But as everyone who lives there will tell you, before you've even asked, sunshine is overrated.

After the list debacle, we settled into one of those chilly, noncommunicative phases that married couples sometimes have when both people are upset but not ready to argue. During that phase, Mike found a job that he wanted and applied for it. I guess he figured I might come around. So we checked it out. We took the kids. Anthony came along to babysit. And for a few days, Seattle looked *very* promising. The city was much prettier than I had expected. It had really nice museums and an aquarium. We drank some good wine, ate some fresh fish, and took in some humidity.

Then, on our last day there, I picked up some of the kids' clothes that I had tossed into a pile on the hotel room floor. They were covered in mold. I started to cry; we left, and never went back.

The moldy clothes wouldn't have been cause for ruling out the entire city if I had otherwise felt great about it. I just didn't. Specifically, I didn't want to leave the rat race in New York—the place we called home, a place we still loved—only to drop ourselves into a *slightly slower* rat race that wasn't much closer to family. I hadn't yet read Maria Semple's *Where'd You Go, Bernadette?*, a hilarious account of Seattle parents who make their own green juice and hover around their kids' schools like gnats, but I knew plenty of people like "Mandy" who were already reeling from its "cutthroat, holier-than-thou, dog-obsessed, health-addict" culture.

After Seattle, and partly because of it, something shifted. That year, two close friends of mine both left New York and moved back to their hometowns. One was Justine, my old Corner Bistro buddy. She was from San Francisco, and her parents, her sister, and grandmother still lived in the area. But that was San Francisco. Moving back to my hometown was something I'd never wanted. In fact, I felt like it was anathema to my adult identity. *New York is where I'm a grown-up.* That's *the place where I found myself. Not the Midwest. Ew.*

Over time, though—like items on a menu that I scrutinized and rejected—all of the other prospects fell away. And Madison, Wisconsin, met a lot of my criteria. Maybe it even predetermined my criteria. While I wasn't psyched about moving back there, it did objectively address several of the problems we faced. It got high scores as a family-friendly town. The *New York Daily News* rated it one of the top one hundred best places to visit. Livability .com ranked it one of the top five best places to live. The public schools were pretty consistently decent. My parents still lived there and, as far as I could tell, were patiently waiting for us to show up.

All I had to do was get Mike on board. Also: find him a job, talk him out of his love of the ocean, and convince him that "hellishly cold winter" was just a phrase that Wisconsin folks use to keep the population down.

POSSIBLY THE MOST COMMON STRATEGY: ARGUE
UNTIL SOMEONE GIVES UP!

In a relationship, it's important to foster common ground. I know this because Mike and I had a couples therapist, and that's what he always said.

"This week," Gil would say, "make sure you say something nice about each other every day." Sometimes Gil gave us such basic advice, it made me wonder if we were even more fucked up than we thought. But the truth is, even couples who want to compromise can find themselves falling down an emotional rabbit hole. Some problems are more intractable than others. We went about our business, in that "terrible limbo" of knowing we had to leave. We'd ignore the impasse, then on the weekend, someone would bring it up again. We'd yell a little. Someone would cry. Usually me. When Mike got really frustrated, he stormed off to work, which made sense because he usually had to be there anyway.

During this time period, Mike and I had at least one extremely rough discussion in which one of us may have deployed the d-word. As a technique for building common ground, this did not meet with Gil's approval. But it happened. It was happening. The decision drove us to the edge of self-doubt and made me wonder if our marriage could actually survive the strain of moving. We had spent so much time arguing about leaving, it almost started to feel easier to leave each other.

Spoiler alert! We stayed together. Gil definitely helped, though the main factor was that Mike found a job. Also, I wore him down. I didn't think my goals were better than his or that I deserved more say in the decision. I wish the process had been more peaceful for both of us. But I am stubborn and combative by nature, and Mike is a diplomatic peacemaker. He likes to say that the only time he knows for sure when he's won an argument is when I stop talking. I almost did, in Seattle. But then the moldy clothes happened and I couldn't step over the line.

Not long after we moved to Wisconsin, I went to a spa with my sister where we met a man from India. During a conversation about cooking, I told him that I had once made garam masala from scratch. It's a common spice blend, he said, available at any grocery store. Why didn't I just buy it? I know, I told him. It's just that once I get an idea in my head, it's hard for me to give up and let it go.

"Ah, I see now," the man said. "You are a difficult person."

Reader, I can't tell you which strategy will work best for you. I wish I could. If you don't have a headhunter or a coin to flip, try the list. Do the yoga and whiskey or whatever. Call Gil, he's in the phone book. Or even keep a gratitude journal. Do whatever works for you. See, the problem with self-help programs is that in real life, one size almost never fits all. People are so different. Even inside the same marriage. In the end, I don't think you can get through a big decision like this without having some hard conversations and fighting it out until someone stops talking.

PART TWO

Settling In

Chapter 4

IT'S THE END OF THE WORLD
AS YOU KNOW IT, AND YOU
HAVE QUESTIONS

QUESTION 1: HOW WILL THE KIDS ADJUST?

If you got one big takeaway from the previous chapter, it should be this: Big life transitions do not have to cause an identity crisis. But they *totally* always do. So just fucking deal with it and move to Seattle.

Or try the other options I suggested. I can't promise any of these options will work for you. As I said, I'm not a positive person, and I don't need to fix you to make myself feel better. That's why I didn't write a self-help manual for tidying up your room. I do sincerely hope that before you move you'll say good-bye to all of those baggy, ripped undies you've held on to for years "just in case." Underwear rationing isn't a thing. Take that spark of joy and run with it.

Having said that, I hope my suggestions are helpful because leaving your home is a slightly bigger deal than underpants purging. If major transitions didn't force people to question their purpose in life, man-losers wouldn't reach forty and suddenly need much younger wives. And really, if *anything* can throw you into an emotional state that feels like a midlife crisis, it's leaving a city full of mood-lit bars and multicultural hipsters and moving to a place where people drive six hours north to a densely wooded lodge on "vacation," where the only thing to see, besides floating loons, is a couple of white guys trying to stuff a dead deer into the backseat of their Ford Durango. Postscript: This precise scenario explains why so many people choose Seattle.

Don't be surprised if you're still freaking out a little bit when you get to your new place. And when you're freaking out, you may wonder if your kids are, too. Everyone says kids are resilient. That's true, and the best example is how girls finish elementary school alive, despite having been forced to play coed dodgeball. More important, kids are truth tellers. Since they aren't in control of the decisions—and don't know how they're "supposed" to act—you can usually tell how they really feel. As you quietly struggle with your identity and existential angst, your kids will articulate—loudly and without caution, in a public place—exactly why you feel that way. They're like canaries, but they're easier to lose because you're not allowed to keep them in a cage.

Our kids were just shy of four and two when we moved, but I worried about how they'd adjust. They were leaving all their friends, a much-beloved babysitter, and a school that—although it obviously wasn't Brearley—they nonetheless liked quite a bit. The older one, in particular, was such a city kid.

Every year since she was born, we had rented a house on Long Island so she could experience the pleasure of playing on a plot of grass that wasn't coated in dog pee, and eating in a kitchen in which we could all sit at the same time.

We'd left the city to visit the grandparents before. But visiting a place doesn't give you the real feels. Most of the time, you visit on holidays. You sit around the house in pajamas and play Jenga with your cousins and argue with your racist uncle. But you don't roam around your hometown, with abundant free time, just to take in the local vibe.

ON LONG ISLAND, we always rented a place on the North Fork, because it was easy to get there very late on a Friday night, after Mike didn't leave work early. Unlike the South Fork—which has tiki beach parties, organic roadside fruit stands, and celebrity megamansions—the North Fork has an outlet mall, a West Nile virus research lab, and a nuclear power plant.

To be fair, it's a defunct nuclear power plant. After years of construction, local residents concluded that clean energy wasn't worth the cost of a potentially botched evacuation. Because to evacuate Long Island—without the private helicopter, from the South Fork—you have to travel sixty miles west, cross Manhattan, and get through a tunnel to the mainland. I was once stuck in a traffic jam in the Lincoln Tunnel for so long that I had to pull a diaper out of my kids' diaper bag and pee into it. Escape a nuclear meltdown? You can't pack enough diapers for that shit.

The very last place we rented before we left New York was in a town called Jamesport. We got there late on Friday, of course, and the property owner was waiting for us on his stoop. He unlocked the door, kindly helped us bring in our bags, showed us around, and, once he was satisfied that we weren't weirdos who peed into diapers, he gave us the keys and left. At which point, our older daughter came out of the bedroom, looked around, and yelled up at me: "WHERE DID THE DOORMAN GO?!"

She wasn't a dummy. Or spoiled. It was just that in her limited experience, grown men who stood *outside* a building and helped you *inside* a building were employed by it.

When we left New York for good, the canary squawked again. Our first summer in Wisconsin, she invented another imaginary person. This one wasn't a strongman from the circus or a fake doorman. It was a little girl and her name was Jazzy Snortskin.

Jazzy didn't live with us. In fact, she didn't live inside at all. She lived in the trees, like a sort of mythological dryad. She sometimes came in to play but Jazzy was her own keeper, and generally speaking, she didn't follow the basic protocols of suburban life. For example, she *never* rode in the car. She rode on top of it. I used to imagine her sitting up on the roof, the wind pinning back her hair while she held fast to the radio antenna. I was really glad she never fell off. Honestly, I'm not sure I would have stopped.

I don't know if my kid invented Jazzy to help her process her new environment or escape from it. Maybe she just needed something to distract her from the fact that she was trapped in a car with her depressing, homesick mother. But that's what I love most about kids. They don't try to hide their identity crisis or stifle their confusion about where the doorman went. Instead of pretending like she totally fit into this weird, wooded environment where people drove their own cars and ate dinner together in the same kitchen, my kid made up a Jazzy theme song, which she'd scream at the top of her lungs, like she was possibly angry about having to cope with so much change.

Then she got over it. Because kids are resilient.

QUESTION 2: DO STEREOTYPES EXIST FOR A REASON?

When you're trying to settle in, stereotypes can be problematic. Writer Karen Karbo made this point eloquently in her review of Meghan Daum's novel, *The Quality of Life Report*. Daum's book is about (among many other things) the shallowness of midwestern stereotypes. "It's the classic misguided fantasy of big-city dwellers everywhere," Karbo wrote in her review, "to flee the crowds, the astronomical rents, the impossible traffic, the crime, the takeout dinners in plastic containers and set down roots in some bucolic locale where the meals are home-cooked and life is never anything but Simple and Good."

Both of these women are fantastic writers, and I stand with them against hurtful stereotypes. But when we first moved, this critique of midwestern stereotypes made no sense to me. If life in Wisconsin didn't seem entirely "simple," it seemed a *helluva* lot simpler than life in New York City! On a good day in Central Park, an investment banker on a racing bike might run a red light, crash into your stroller, and send your limp lifeless baby flying into a cart of hot nuts. Life in Madison was . . . slower. Our first summer here, the local newspaper featured stories like "Floral Door Wreaths You'll Love" and "Canoe Enthusiast Takes Action." Mike didn't even know you could use *canoe* and *action* in the same sentence!

If you don't believe me, ask Oprah. She has a home up here. I'm pretty sure the only reason she sent her scientists to Papua New Guinea was that she couldn't convince them to drive north to study the primitive people of Wisconsin. But no matter, because I'm here to tell you about them. From the minute we arrived, the number of weekly conversations we had about quilting went from zero to five. And *oh boy* do people here knit. They do it in public. Like, anywhere, anytime. People also still use snowshoes, mostly for fun, but also for transportation. Because how else would they explore the ice caves on Lake Superior, amirite?

These kinds of stereotypes feed off real regional differences. I spoke with a woman named "Laura" who grew up in Brooklyn but eventually relocated to a bedroom community in the Los Angeles area. Stereotypically speaking, people complain about traffic and overpopulation there pretty much nonstop. But according to Laura, a big part of the problem is that people don't move fast enough. "The lines move so slowly and nobody seems to mind," she told me in her Brooklyn accent. "A quick trip to Rite Aid can take thirty minutes! People are waiting on line, relaxed and smiling, while my body twitches." Coming from New York, Laura didn't understand how people in such a crowded place could be so laid-back and poky. Because meanwhile, she said, they fulfilled every California stereotype about kids and devices: "The school allows cell phones to be used between class periods and at lunch . . . WTF?!"

Like food—which I will address later in the program—traffic patterns are easy to stereotype. No matter where we drove in this town, we noticed, it took between eight and fifteen minutes. In New York, it took us fifteen minutes just to get our car out of the garage! The way people drive is different, too. Like, let's say you're going to a knitting expo to get some special yarn and you have to get into a left turn lane. Those hot-to-trot knitters will line up for blocks, single file, and *wait their turn*. All we have to do is speed up, do an end run around the line, and cut in at the front. Because in New York, that's called merging! We felt a little guilty doing it here, at first, but we never get merge-shamed because people here are also too polite to honk. Sorry, not sorry.

In pointing out real cultural differences, I don't want to reinforce any dirty rotten stereotypes. But when I was first getting my bearings, I often wondered, *Don't some stereotypes exist for a reason?* Maybe that sounds gross, but dig this, Judge Judies. In New York, we lived on the twelfth floor of a high-rise co-op. Our bedroom windows looked north, toward Harlem and the Bronx. It was buildings and motor vehicles as far as the eye could see. Far off in the distance, near the Triborough Bridge, we could see the glowing red billboard that advertised the History Channel. Our kid called it the "Red Thing," pointing up at it every night like it was the moon. I say it was *like* the moon because she couldn't see the real moon. You can't typically see celestial bodies from a high-rise. Stereotypically speaking, city kids aren't real outdoorsy. They stargaze at neon billboards.

I grew up in a more outdoorsy culture. My childhood home, for example, is nestled on a quiet cul-de-sac on the south side of a small lake. *Cul-de-sac* makes it sound quaint; in fact, the signs at both ends of the street just say DEAD END. But anyway, in the wintertime, when that lake is frozen, men sit out there in tents and wooden shelters and fish through holes in the ice. Several years ago, my dad had to tear down his boathouse, not because it was falling apart or because he sold his pontoon boat, but because ice fishermen kept breaking into it and pooping in the spare tires.

When we started looking for a house, we had to keep stuff like this in mind. Not fisherman dung, but, like, how alienated from nature we had become. Neither of us wanted to live out in the corn-burbs, with the heated garages and the seated lawn mowers and the zombie children. Mike actually preferred a more "urban" neighborhood, meaning there was a grocery store within walking distance and you didn't have to be friends with your neighbors. I longed for a tighter-knit community. One place we both liked had community and walkability—it was a quiet residential neighborhood with a good public school and a nearby grocery store. But the real estate agent kept giving us the hard sell on how it was "heavily wooded." I was like, what now? On a good day, woods make me think of *The Blair Witch Project*. On a bad day—like a cold, overcast, sideways-snowing one—I'm pretty sure I'll end up like that dude in *The Revenant* who was attacked by a bear and forced to take shelter inside a hollowed-out horse.

When we finally bit the bullet and bought a home in the haunted forest, though, some things about it were *so* much simpler. Like after twenty years of schlepping dirty laundry hither and yon, we had our own laundry room. I'm not talking about a closet with a washing machine like we had in the condo, Reader, I'm talking a *whole room*. Was this "room" really just the utility corner of a damp cellar? Why yes, it was. But it was better than loading the laundry onto an elevator and dodging rats in the basement of our apartment building! It was even better than having laundry right inside your cramped apart-ment. Because in New York, that is often less glamorous than it sounds. For a long time, my friend Michelle couldn't even do her laundry in the evening hours without her downstairs neighbor complaining about the noise. In Wisconsin, we could do the laundry *whenever it was dirty*.

That laundry room was a magical gift that kept on giving! First, I got an expandable drying rack and left it open all the time, without blocking access to the dryer. Then one day, I ran out of detergent, and instead of having to throw both kidlings into a double stroller and push them four blocks to the local bodega—uphill and in the rain—I just hopped into the car and drove to the nearest Target. Which had a Starbucks. *Inside of it.* While I was roaming around in there, I picked up a few stackable plastic baskets for no good reason, then went home and put a bunch of random hats in them. All of this laundry toiling took less than an hour. I couldn't wait to fold it!

The only thing that was simpler and better than the laundry room was *everything*. Our house was three times as big as our New York apartment and cost half as much. We got a jungle gym for the backyard so the kids could play outside—again, *whenever* they felt like it. We bought bikes and ice skates and a hot mess of sports equipment to clutter up the garage. The guy who built our fence sold us his used lawn mower, which made us feel both handy *and* thrifty. We put out the American flag that was left by the previous owners, in the flag holder they had installed. Our house looked so patriotic. Around the corner, there was a public elementary school. Registration took fifteen minutes, involved no interviews, and everyone in the district was accepted.

Simple? Good? Yes, ma'am. It was the new reality equivalent of having a pillow fight while walking barefoot in a field of fresh-cut grass and eating a homemade cookie.

QUESTION 3: WHY DIDN'T WE MOVE HERE *YEARS* AGO?

Right now, you may be asking yourself: Is it even safe to eat a cookie during a pillow fight? And that's a great question. While stereotypes can have some basis in reality, it's also true that when you're in the middle of a life transition to a new place, you may be seeing a more superficial—idealized—version of reality. The human brain can't take in all that much detail, all that accurately, all at once. That is especially true when you're under stress, trying desperately to convince yourself that the words "heavily wooded" don't terrify you.

I spoke to a woman named "Abby," for example, who relocated from the Midwest to Denver for her husband's job. She wanted to live in a diverse, older neighborhood, but with twin school-age boys, she needed a bigger house, close to her husband's office and a public school. After renting for a year, they ended up buying a house in a suburban community where, according to Abby, "everyone is in exactly the same stage of life, has two to four kids, and is midcareer." It wasn't diverse, or historic. But having all those kids around made the relocation much easier. "There was no 'groove' to fit in," Abby said. "Everyone was so accepting of new neighbors!"

Reader, if you feel skeptical about Abby's use of the word *everyone*—twice in the same paragraph—let me say that it's this kind of critical thinking that makes you an unrivaled book-reading champion. I understood where Abby was coming from, because I felt exactly that way after we moved. Adults aren't like kids. We can't adjust to a new place by imagining new friends who ride on top of the car and somehow never fall off.

We have to imagine entire communities. We have to imagine perfection.

And I truly was so relieved at how easy it was to assimilate into our new community. Our new neighborhood had so many fun things to do! None of those things were a natural history museum, a Broadway musical, or being dabbed by Dick Cavett. But we did have a centrally located public school, an outdoor neighborhood pool, and a community garden. In wintertime, they made a skating rink on the village green, so Mike could fall down on ice at least once a year. Every Fourth of July, the volunteer firefighters sponsored a neighborhood party complete with an egg toss, a fire hose battle, and a Popsicle-eating contest. We even had a village forester, which is evidently a real thing, to take care of the forest.

We stayed mindful of the trade-offs. Letting go of the dream that my kids would grow up as snobby coastal elites didn't happen overnight. At best, they might land a minor role in a children's theater production of *Fiddler on the Roof* and get written up in a local paper for their empathetic portrayal of Yente. And that is not nothing, because Yente is a challenging role. More important, Mike had left a good job and a salary he'd worked hard for years to get. Would our family suffer that 80 percent salary cut? Should we get rid of our AmEx card? Do the stores here even take AmEx?

And the moving itself wasn't all fun and games. It was also no fun and no games. Shortly after we escaped the condo in the cornfield, Mike ruptured his Achilles tendon playing pickup basketball. He was in a lot of pain. Since I had to unpack and pack all our shit by myself—for the second time, since Mike had pioneered it out here—I wasn't very helpful to him. Even then, those challenges didn't overtake the simple, good stuff. We had a two-minute drive to the hospital, and a top-notch medical team. People he hardly knew from his office offered to pick him up and drive him to work. "Honey!" I said to Mike one day, as he hobbled out the door by himself. "I feel like we moved to one of those fifties TV places where people sit on their front porches and wave at random strangers walking down the street."

Again, that sounds like a stereotype. But that's how it was, and I was charmed! When our friend Mark came out to visit, he said the exact same thing! Being a New Yorker, Mark is accustomed to barreling down the sidewalk looking straight ahead with a determined look on his face so nobody asks him for money or drugs or directions. In New York, they just call that walking. One day during his visit to Wisconsin, we all took a bike ride and guess what happened. A random guy in a random yard waved to us! I was feeling it. I actually waved back!

"Wow," Mark said. "That was such a Mayberry moment."

Mark was referring to *good* Mayberry, of course, the one with the local barber and the diner and the hapless but lovable town drunkard, not the *bad* one, with whitevangelical patriarchy and the Ku Klux Klan. But it was an apt term, and we nestled deep into that Americana. In the middle of the summer, we went to the traditional water ballet show at the community pool, where the swim team has a dunk tank for charity and some committee of local villagers sponsors an ice cream social. No, you heard me: *an ice cream social*. With big brown tubs of locally made ice cream scooped up by volunteers. It was like

Mayberry meets *Toddlers & Tiaras*, but without the creepy pageant moms.

Inspired by my renewed sense of civic belonging, I actually joined the scooping group. It was called the Village League. Privately, Mike and I referred to it as the Village League of Peace and Justice, because who uses the word *League* anymore, besides bowlers and cartoonists? But I didn't share that with the league ladies. At my second meeting, at the house of a neighbor I didn't know, I drank a smidge too much and dropped a wineglass on the kitchen floor. It shattered. The hostess just got me another glass and offered me some squares of cheese. She didn't even seem mad! She just cleaned it up! Herself!

We went so native, Reader, we even got a Subaru. We had one car already and we kept it, because it was five years old and only had forty thousand miles on it. Thanks, New York. But in the burbs you need ALL THE CARS. Around here, the two most obvious choices were a Subaru or a minivan.

Being clever coastal types, we quickly reckoned that minivans are the highest form of suburban transportation. They're like the Clydesdale horse of family vehicles: spacious, sturdy, and reliable, and unlike SUVs, they don't cost a lot of money or guzzle that much gas. In the burbs, you can drive a shitload of kids around, along with their ice skates, hockey bags, swim bags, soccer bags, soccer chairs, backpacks, some garden manure, some garden gnomes, a jumbo pack of paper towels, and several large tubs of macadamia nut clusters from Costco. Never mind that the second you get behind the wheel of a minivan, you feel like you're sixty-four years old. So what, who cares? You didn't move here because you're young.

The woman across the street stumped for the van. She had a cautionary tale about the Subaru. Basically, everything was clicking along without a hitch until her daughter got kicked out of the tennis team car pool because she couldn't pool enough kids in there. Oh snap! They booted her out like a pickup artist working the room at a women's convention. They were totally Wisconsin-nice about it, though.

We got the Subaru anyway, because getting dumped by the car pool didn't seem that bad to me, and it definitely was better than feeling old. And in the suburbs, you drive around *all day long.* You drive to the grocery store. You drive to the bank. You drive to your friend's house. You can even drive to a drive-through coffee shop and wait in a car line with the engine running while they make you a drink. The Subaru had front cup holders and backseat cup holders for the kids' juice boxes or whatever, and I was into it. Driving with cup holders was the literal opposite of taking the subway. It was so simple and convenient, I almost wanted to get a gratitude journal just to write about it.

Our new lifestyle wasn't spellbinding or anything, but the suburbs were turning out to be simple *and* pretty good. We jumped in like kids near a dirty ball pit. Fitness through raking! More Target stores than people! Ice cream socials run by lady superheroes! An entire garage just for storing unused sports equipment! Backseat cup holders and drive-through coffee shops! *Yippee!* I thought to myself as the garage door closed automatically behind me and Jazzy Snortskin climbed onto the bike rack. *This isn't the end of the world! It's Norwegian Fucking Fantasy Island!*

Our pastoral fantasy was midwestern. But the same small-town celebration was happening, in real time, throughout the country. Shortly after she left the city, "Carolyn" told me that she really loved suburban Connecticut. No matter where she went in her new town, there was *always* a parking space. I heard a similar sentiment from "Ruby" when she moved to Arizona. Coming from New York, she couldn't believe how lazy everyone seemed. "No one ever got out of their cars," she observed. That's what she saw, and that's how she felt, right up until she settled in and started using "every damn drive-up" she could access and "loving every minute of it."

We should've left New York years ago! Quick, someone call Madonna and tell her to move back to the Midwest! Ol' Blue Eyes was right. You *can* make it anywhere!

Chapter 5

CULTURE SHOCK IS REAL

SEVERAL MONTHS IN, you are *crushing it*! Pretty much everybody—including the drive-thru barista and the pretend girl on top of the car—thinks you're an awesome decider. In the history of always, definitely probably nobody has ever made a smoother transition.

I get it. That's how I felt as we continued to settle into our new reality. The kids saw their dad at dinnertime now, instead of just first thing in the mornings. With another parent home in the evenings, I was finally able to enroll in a continuing education class to learn Spanish, which I'd been too busy to do for a long time. That first summer, I went twice a week in the evenings—until Mike injured his leg, anyway. Then I had to quit. *Qué pena*, I thought, wishing I knew what that meant.

Even without the Spanish language skills, however, I was thrilled with our choice. I wholeheartedly embraced the slower pace of suburban Wisconsin. I commandeered that Subaru around town like a boss! I never had to wait for a train or a taxi. I could just get in my wagon, pop a drink in my cup holder, and drive on out of my garage. And the scenery was so friendly and quaint. Like the flags! They had orange safety flags on the corners of certain main streets, which pedestrians carried as they crossed to increase their visibility. The main streets didn't look that busy to me. And I didn't really grasp the science behind why drivers would stop for a flag and not an actual person. But these clever crossing guards had obviously figured it out. Visibility now! Safety first! *It was perfect.*

Or was it?

(SCREECH SOUND EFFECT.)

Reader, I've been pretty candid up until now. I gave you the straight talk about the curveballs and the failure. I told you about the time I slept on a Milk Dud and then ate it. I didn't even hold back about the diaper incident in the traffic jam, and that's not a moment I'm particularly proud of. But on the topic of your perfect transition, I've been leading you astray just a teensy weensy bit. I've been hinting that the good feels might last forever, that those first impressions were solid, and that we were standing on bedrock with those cultural stereotypes. Maybe you knew that wasn't the end of the story, because it all seemed too easy, and stereotypes are not okay, and also, there are still a bunch of pages left. Either way, it's time for me to come clean.

Stereotypes aren't always totally false, but they are always incomplete. You can float down the river of generalizations for quite a while, happily snacking on spreadable cheese and forty-ounce wine coolers, but after a few weeks or months on that drunken raft, your eyes start to adjust to the light and the scenery comes into sharper focus. As more data points come in, you get a more complete picture. And now, with the full Monty of your new reality in plain sight, you suspect that you maybe weren't quite the suburban boss you believed yourself to be.

Reader, welcome to culture shock.

Culture shock is a state of confusion and disorientation that happens when you immerse yourself in an unfamiliar way of life. You may have felt it before, like when you were a kid and your parents took you to Florida, and you saw old men wearing sun hats and homemade shell jewelry, and realized that nothing in your cultural vocabulary could possibly explain whatever this was.

Or maybe you felt it in college, when you went overseas and an Egyptian man reached into his jogging shorts and pulled out his hot little lamb kebab. Then a few months later, some dude on a Spanish park bench reached underneath his crossword puzzle and pulled out his stubby pencil. Since you'd never been to these places before—and you hadn't seen the numbers on what percentage of skulking men were certifiable pervs—you just ran away and decided it was 100.

I know what you're thinking. What do foreign perverts have to do with leaving my cool city? I'm not living in a park in Madrid! I have a cool Subaru, son! Well, it can happen anywhere, and to anyone. It can affect people who leave Houston, San Francisco, or Rochester. It can definitely happen if you leave New York—one of the most vibrant culinary scenes in the world—and move to a place where people call garlic a "spicy food" and the two main cooking seasons are grilling and Crock-Pot.

But in the beginning, you don't even know you're experiencing culture shock, because you're in the first phase: the Honeymoon.

I hate to get too technical, but I have to hit you with some information. Culture shock has four phases: Honeymoon, Judgment, Adjustment, and the ultimate goal of Mastery. We'll touch on all of them eventually. Does adjusting to and then mastering your move mean you'll get to the new place, immediately love ice fishing, and/or start pooping in tires? Not necessarily. Does it mean keeping an open mind to new experiences, listening to locals when they talk about ice fishing, and then deciding—based on all the available data points—to stay inside where there is natural gas, and an actual toilet? Probably. Getting comfortable enough to accept—or reject—a certain way of life can take months. Or, if you're as emotionally chaotic as I am, possibly several years. But true fact: We all start with the Honeymoon phase.

THE HONEYMOON PHASE

If you've ever gone on an actual honeymoon, I hope it was fun. On my honeymoon, I was stung by a sea urchin and showered with rain forest pesticide. I was also visibly pregnant, which made those first two things even worse. Years later, I was interviewed by a *New York Times* reporter for an article about people who suck at taking honeymoons and reading it later, we did sound legitimately stupid.

For most people, though, honeymoons are supposed to be fun. Nobody expects you to do anything but drink and eat and have sex. Unless you are pregnant and get stung by a sea urchin, you don't have to visit a local hospital. You don't even have to leave your fucking hotel room. If anything in the world is simple and good, it's a honeymoon.

But a honeymoon—much like the pastoral midwestern stereotype—isn't entirely real. It may contain nuggets of truth, but not the whole truth. On my honeymoon, for example, we did eat delicious fruit. We also napped a bit and walked through a festive outdoor market that featured hanging meats. After the sea urchin debacle, Mike held on to my hand whenever we went snorkeling, to protect me from further oceanic peril. Those two factors—eating and making my husband swim next to me—have defined most of our married life and I'm not sorry.

Yet, actual marriage is more complicated than a honeymoon. It's only after you're settled into your marital home—and life returns to its regular heart-racing pace—that you emerge from your weird honeymoon trance. Then you're like, wait, I bought a CD of that mariachi band? I don't even like mariachi! I've had a sensory disorder my entire life. Oh my God, why is that trumpet so *loud*?!

Moving is the same. Some of us are more easily amused than others, but if you got as excited about stackable laundry baskets as you did about that mariachi music, then all the data points were probably *not* in. Reader, those baskets might make life easier—because you don't have to root around in the closet to find a random hat—but they are not enough. Like, you can love your husband. So much. But you still need girlfriends. Because every once in a while, you crave the company of someone who knows the difference between snuggling and sexy time.

Here's what actually happens in the Honeymoon phase. In our haste to settle in, we celebrate the novelties. It's human nature to enjoy new experiences. We also enjoy them because we want to fit in. Like when Mike first got here and wanted to learn how to cross-country ski. After one lesson with me, he took the skis off and didn't speak to me for three days. Or like when

I went to garden club with my mom, learned what a "perennial" was, and decided I was going to be a gardener. The moment I did some actual gardening, and I realized it was mostly weeding, I should've admitted to myself that I'd rather just stay inside and watch bunnies eat my tulips while I had a cocktail. But I still did it for a while, because honeymoons.

Also, you just can't know everything about a place right away. Things that seem fun when they're new can feel very different in a few months, when you fully delve into them. That's when you *really* have questions. Once you step out of the enchanted bubble of the Honeymoon phase, you may begin to wonder whether driving around all day in a Subaru is *actually* the meaning of life. Wait, am I going to have to pull weeds *every* year? Does anyone ever find *anything* they are shopping for at Home Depot?

On my first trip to the Depot, I wandered through the aisles with a shit-eating grin on my face. I couldn't find anyone to help me, but I didn't care. I was just so pumped to be walking around in a store the size of Grand Central Terminal, with nobody running into me! After living in so many apartments with crumbly plaster walls, the drywall was so dazzling. And garden supplies? In the same store? Keep Manhattan, just give me that countryside!

Yeah, well, *one* trip to Home Depot is a novelty. Make four consecutive trips there in a week—for window cranks, a weather radio, floodlight bulbs, and outdoor extension cords that are somehow always the wrong length—and you start to see the downside. You may discover that, in fact, you can't ever find anyone to help you. Nobody in that vast orange wasteland of part-time labor is, in fact, ever able to answer questions related to products, pricing, availability, or location. Most of them appear to be wandering the aisles, just like you are, completely lost. And can you really blame them? The store is the size of Grand Fucking Central.

My nature crush followed a similar narrative arc. For most of my adult life, my experience of foliage was restricted to strolling through Central Park with a cute scarf, a pair of leather riding boots, and an everything bagel. At the end of our first summer in Wisconsin, our neighborhood started looking super L.L. Bean, in terms of both fashion and scenery. I was getting used to the scary forest, and I was loving it! After a few more garden club meetings, I had pretty much decided I was a tree whisperer. A few weeks into autumn, after raking the leaves upward of twenty times, it suddenly dawned on me that living under the trees—rather than just walking past them on the way to a museum—is an epic pain in the peacoat.

It took a while to learn this lesson. The first time Mike got up on a ladder to clean leaves out of the gutter, I was like, *Yaasss, Paul Bunyan!* I was holding a ladder, Mike was doing his lumbersexual, gutter-jockey thing. We've never done this much manual labor in our lives! We have mad skillz now! But eventually, that appeal wore off. Know why? Because the fucking leaves keep on falling! Halfway into the month of October, I started dreading the rain, because it meant we'd have to schlep that damn ladder to the back porch—*again*—and scrape decomposing plant garbage out of the gutters. And it's not like you can wear cute leather riding boots out in that mess! You need waterproof work boots! What was I going to find out next— that Paul Bunyan wasn't even a real lumberjack?

Reader, this kind of disillusionment is what signals the end of the Honeymoon phase. In some cases, it phases out gradually. In others, it ends with a single, dramatic event. Nobody can speak to this better than our dear friend "Abby."

Recall that when Abby relocated to Denver, she found a home in a sparkly new suburb with lots of families and felt very welcome. For the first few weeks, she said, it was "all Kumbaya." Neighbors were coming over a lot, and being solicitous. But over time, she noticed that everyone shut their shades all the time for privacy. They seemed to have a special way of talking which she described as "not rude, but not a real conversation." The Pilates moms kept their rock-solid core muscles—and their social circle—pretty tight. As nuances emerged, people gossiped about who set off the loud fireworks or who had the barking dog, and she noticed that many of these neighbors weren't actually that fond of each other. She hung in there with the positive attitude. Until the entire façade crumbled.

After a few months, Abby's son began asking why he and his brother kept knocking on friends' doors, but never got invited inside. "He knew he wasn't in the inner circle," Abby explained, but it wasn't clear why. One day, Abby heard through the grapevine that her closest neighbor found her kids annoying. Back in the Midwest, their neighbors had been very relaxed about impromptu playdates. They were casual and comfortable about letting their kids come over. When she thought about it, she realized she had imported this attitude to Colorado. But the new place didn't actually have the same free-form culture. After a few incidents like this—in which her kids got rejected, or she heard a negative comment—Abby felt really bad. She'd been unpacking, she told me, and not paying close attention. The neighborhood was filled with families, but was it actually family *friendly*? From that point on, she set up playdates in advance, and started talking to neighbors over the fence like everyone else.

On the topic of faux-friendly, I also talked to "Christopher," a thirtysomething single man who moved from Illinois to Wisconsin to work for a newspaper. He looked forward to living in Madison because it was twice as big as his hometown. He had read somewhere (he wasn't sure where) that it was "one of the five gay friendliest cities in the country." He liked the restaurant and museum scenes. Yet he "was hard-pressed to locate other gay men, outside of the bars." It was a tolerant place, Christopher found, but gay culture was by no means thriving. His honeymoon bubble finally burst when he went on his first date. The guy took him to LongHorn Steakhouse, a mediocre chain restaurant behind a shopping mall. During the meal, Christopher discovered the guy was closeted, or, as he sarcastically put it, "not yet gay friendly." Christopher decided he would have to adjust his "cosmopolitan standards" to survive dating there.

Nothing shuts down a projected fantasy like the whole truth. But a bird carcass works pretty well, too. I discovered this one day, when a small yellow bird crashed into my living room window. It left a wet smear mark, with feathers stuck to it, then dropped onto the back porch. Since I had just finished setting up a bird-feeding station in my backyard, I felt kind of dejected. My mom gave me some story about how birds got confused in the autumn, because of "declining light" or something. All I knew was that a member of my flock had bit the big one right outside my living room and—more importantly—nobody else was home to clean it up.

I brainstormed some solutions. My first thought was to call Alfredo, our former apartment superintendent, whose number was still in my phone. But I dismissed that idea as impractical: It would take him days to get here, even if he left right now. So I looked in the village directory and called a neighbor. He picked up the phone right away, like he'd just been sitting there, warming up his slow cooker. I hit him with a heavy artillery of questions. *Do birds carry avian flu? Do they have ticks? Do they have rabies? Should I use rubber gloves? Also, I never did find gardening gloves at Home Depot; can I borrow some?*

I'm not going to lie to you, Reader, I wanted him to come over and remove the carcass for me. He didn't, and that was a real disappointment. I mean, my mom hadn't offered to do it, either, but she lived across town. He lived right next door, it was two o'clock in the afternoon, and I knew for a fact that the only items on his to-do list that day—other than cooking down that stew beef—were the crossword puzzle and maybe a little Fox News. He couldn't open the back door and toss me some gloves? What kind of non-Mayberry shit was that? Instead, he mumbled something about a shovel. "Just throw the bird away," he said. "Put it in a plastic bag and toss it in the bin." Fine, I thought. These are the hazards of country living. This is the price of adventure. But then—just to taunt me, probably because he hates the Yankees— he dropped this info-nugget: "Just use a single bag. If it were a deer carcass, of course, you'd have to double bag it."

As I scooped up the bird with a pasta fork, I experienced a slew of unpleasant emotions. I tried to focus on the facts. Bird. Bag. Trash. I reasoned that we probably lived too close to the center of town for big-game hunting, but I felt disoriented and confused. *I'm sorry*, I thought to myself, *did he just say DEER*

CARCASS? Is a DEER CARCASS something that could conceivably appear in my backyard? I wanted the kids to be exposed to nature, not *The Hunger Games.* First the fake news about Paul Bunyan . . . now *this?*

That's how it goes down. With each new experience, the stereotypical simplicity of your new life becomes more nuanced. Late that summer, for instance, another neighbor brought us zucchini from her garden. I was overwhelmed with gratitude. Getting fresh, locally grown vegetables delivered in a bicycle basket? How totally quaint is that! And also, how impressive! The only vegetable garden I'd ever sowed was in college, when my friend John and I volunteered for an amnesty organization that helped Central American refugees. And I should have apologized to those refugees because that garden *sucked.* Eventually, though, I discovered that in Wisconsin, zucchini grows like the plague. It's basically the Ebola of squash. Most people spend the latter part of August trying to pawn their zucchini off on anyone stupid enough to take it, which, that August, was absolutely me.

Mayberry took another hit a few weeks later, when the busybody brigade came out to greet us. Look, I'm not picking on my town when I say this; folks like this exist everywhere. When "Mandy" moved from Seattle back to the Midwest, she couldn't believe all the people who felt perfectly free to comment on her kids' behavior and appearance, her lifestyle, her clothing, her choice of meat, and her ethnicity, which—to make matters worse—they called her "nationality." She "longed for the days of wearing all black," not being the "first *hapa* someone has ever met," and, as I said before, riding an elevator in silence.

"Hilde" moved to Birmingham, Alabama, so her husband, a thyroid surgeon, could take his dream job at the medical school there. It made her feel really weird at first that people kept asking *where* she lived. The general neighborhood was "not enough," she explained to me. "Right when you meet, they want to know exactly which street." Hilde suspected they were sizing up her income and status. She would try to divert the subject with a sarcastic retort like: "Why, are you going to bring me a welcome cake?" All those busybodies, and nobody brought her a single cake.

In my town, the brigade was concerned about my yard. Everyone's yard, really. Weeding seemed to be of paramount concern, and especially the garlic mustard, which was allegedly a very troubling and ruinous weed. I didn't know that because, WTF? But since I didn't want to be a one-woman mustard scourge, I started looking for it. Constantly. I had to ask a work colleague—I was back to working part-time by the end of that summer—to come over and help me identify it. But before I could even address that impending calamity, I saw one of the brigade ladies peering at me from across the street. I waved, and she said, "I just wondered what you're planting back there." I wondered what I was planting back there, too. I also wondered why the garlic mustard–free fuck she cared.

One day—in casual conversation with Mike—the husband of one of the busybodies mentioned that his wife didn't care for our jungle gym, "especially the color of the canopy." Oh, *really*? Funny story: I didn't particularly care for the color of her hair, but I had somehow managed to keep that to myself all these weeks. Mike—who is more peaceable and quicker to compromise than I am—went all the way back to the store and got a new canopy. Did this appease her? Well if it did, we never heard about it. We ultimately decided her real problem was that we had moved in and disrupted her unsullied view of our backyard.

From that point on, the cat was out of the bag. Although we also discovered that it would have been a lot safer in the bag, because some guy in the neighborhood was shooting family pets with a handgun.

Oh my God, I thought.

This place is *simple. In the* bad *Mayberry way.*

THE JUDGMENT PHASE

If you're having thoughts like these, you're squarely in the Judgment phase, which, according to anthropologists, is the unavoidable phase that follows the cultural honeymoon. Everyone goes through it. Whether New Yorkers experience the Judgment phase more intensely than others is hard to say, although experts believe that this phase of culture shock may be difficult to distinguish from their regular pissy attitudes.

You definitely can't avoid the Judgment phase, though, just because you returned to your hometown. I grew up here. I had raked as a kid. Theoretically, I should've been prepared for the annual dumping of the tree garbage. But you forget stuff. And when it comes back to you, it's a flaky kid memory, because kids have low blood sugar a lot, and the rest of the time, they're selfish assholes. When I "raked" as a kid, I made one pile of leaves just big enough so I could jump in it with my siblings. Then, after running through it like twenty or thirty times, the leaves would be spread all over the yard again and I'd go inside for hot apple cider while my dad finished the rest of the raking. Which was all of it. What? I had low blood sugar.

UNLESS YOU ARE Gandhi—and you pretty much just laugh at everything—you should expect to encounter cultural discomfort in a variety of areas during the Judgment phase, including written laws, travel patterns, food, dress codes, communication, social customs, parenting styles, religious beliefs, and political views.

In one particularly awkward communication fiasco, I managed to horrify a woman from up the street simply by being myself. I'd received a care package from my friend Helen, who was one of the founding members of our New York coffee shop breastfeeding group. To my delight, the box contained a smorgasbord of novelty items from Zabar's, including kosher butter cookies shaped like hot dogs, packed in a Chinese takeout container. *Oh, the irony!* I laughed. I cried. I ate cookies. I cried some more. Not quite as hard as I had cried about the moldy clothes in Seattle, but really, really close. The fact that Helen's son sometimes adorably mispronounced our new home as "Misconsin" made me miss her, and New York, even more.

Still sniffling, I ran into the small woman who always wore tennis clothes and frequently walked her designer dog past our house. She asked how I was doing, and that was nice, so I gave her a detailed update.

Everything was great, I answered, but today was hard. I just received a care package from my friend Helen, who was a scientist at Columbia. The box was from Zabar's. It was left on the stoop. The cookies were kosher. Packed in a Chinese takeout container. Ha! Ha! We used to breastfeed together! In public! Ho boy. Good times.

I didn't know if the tennis lady had been fishing for gossip, got none, and got bored or if she suddenly got a phone call from her tennis pro. But right about then, her eyes glazed over like a dead shark, then she abruptly excused herself and walked away.

Puzzled, I sifted back through our exchange. Had I been too needy? Did I use too many ethnic terms? Was she confused by the word *stoop*? Maybe she had never heard about Zabar's and thought I said "rebar." I went home feeling frustrated and lonely. Later, I recounted the episode to a friend, who speculated that this woman was a social conservative who had never lived outside of the state. I wasn't sure that explained her hostility to ethnic food and feminism, but around here you can't be sure. Good thing I didn't mention the Upper Breast Side!

Looking back, that incident perfectly exemplified the Judgment phase. Instead of seeing every interaction with a neighbor as a lighthearted Mayberry moment, I started questioning whether they were offended by me, or vice versa. This downward emotional tumble made me feel defensive. I liked it here, but did I really belong? Whether you live in a small city, a suburb, an exurb, or an all-gay retirement home in Palm Springs, you will naturally evolve toward a recognition that your new culture isn't accommodating all your needs, and then fear that you might never feel truly at home. This negative slide can cause you to become aggressively judgmental about, say, people who decide vaccines aren't safe but still let their sons play football. You're not wrong to judge them, because that's just stupid. But now you're overreacting the other way. Like when your mom sits down to send an e-mail on an old desktop computer, presses delete instead of send, and then declares that the computer is broken. Nope. No, Mom. You're just pressing the wrong buttons.

Eventually, Reader, you'll get past the Judgment phase, just as you did with your honeymoon fantasies. You'll figure out how to negotiate local customs and unspoken rules and language barriers in unique ways that work for you. Part of that negotiation will be adopting what experts call a "spirit of humility" about things you once hated. Part of it will be resilience, and problem solving on the fly. First, however, you do need to confront your strong negative reactions to things you'd previously believed were just simple and good. And quaint. To help you get there, I want to share a few stories taken from my own journey through the Judgment phase, along with some self-helpful insights.

Chapter 6

THE TARGETS OF MY DISCONTENT

I. GROWN-ASS ADULTS DON'T NEED FLAGS.

Last chapter, I told you that children are flaky because they always have low blood sugar. Well, guess what else Dr. Spock taught me: Kids are also short. They don't pay attention. They run when they're supposed to walk. And even when they walk, they zigzag around like the town crackhead. Because of all these things plus low blood sugar, kids maybe need flags to alert drivers that they are crossing the street.

You know who really doesn't, though? A grown-ass man. When I say *man*, I'm not talking about a bent old grandad on his way to the pharmacy. I'm talking about a thirtysomething sociology professor in a knit cap, holding the safety flag up in the air like he's leading an Olympic procession to the home brew supply store. Except it's an Olympic procession of one stinky hippie, because there are no kids in sight. When he gets across, is he also going to lecture me about feminism? C'mon, dude. The only warning flags you need are your bro beard and your man bun.

To be fair, the flag bros were not my only gripe. First of all, the flags seemed unnecessary. The flag buckets were located on corners that didn't have a stoplight. Which makes sense in theory, except those corners were like, a block from corners that did have a stoplight. The more I watched the adult safety parade, the more I had to wonder: Why can't these able-bodied people just walk one more block and cross at the light? Because I just stopped my car back there, at the *stoplight*. Now I have to stop—again—right here? I don't want to ruin your day with a factual counterpoint, hippies, but you do know that stopping wastes gas, right?

Also, the flags seemed kind of extreme. I'm a proponent of safety. That's another way of saying I'm a huge chickenshit, and it's true. I hate roller coasters, and I don't ski because I'm afraid of chairlifts. My profound fearfulness is why I never listen to Buddhists. It's a widely known fact that Buddhists are overly accepting of death, and, therefore, I can't trust them to warn me away from things that might kill me. The same is obviously true of carnies, palliative care doctors, and airline pilots.

I am generally very tolerant of people with fears and phobias because I have them too. I've never heard of a street-crossing phobia, per se, but I can imagine someone being fearful about it because about one in ten people suffer from a crippling fear.

While tolerance is important, however, we can't give in to irrational fears. Do we really want to become a society of militant pedestrians who insist on the right to cross at every single corner? In this town, it turns out, the answer is a resounding yes. College students pretty much step into the road whenever they damn well please. According to the law, cars basically have to stop at *every crosswalk* into which a pedestrian has stepped, is about to step, or is thinking of stepping at some indeterminate point in the future. Some random drunk frat boy could be standing near the curb, daydreaming about rush week, and drivers will slam on the brakes and wait there until he sobers up.

This culture of pedestrian supremacy really started to bug me whenever I had somewhere important to go in this town. And while no example of that type of event comes to mind immediately, I'm sure you get my point.

I'm happy to report that I no longer fly into a rage at the sight of orange flags. First of all, a lot of those flag buckets have been replaced by blinking lights, which don't look as ridiculous. But I had also recognized my aggravation as a classic sign of the Judgment phase. I was annoyed that I had to coddle adult people on the sidewalk! This was definitely a cultural thing in my case, and not just a menopausal mood swing. New York doesn't have what most people would call a "pedestrian-friendly" culture. People do walk *everywhere*. It's a walking city. But people undertake the walking at their own risk. Pedestrians in New York have almost no aversion to stepping into a busy street—an actually busy street: Broadway at Fifty-Seventh, for example—in front of oncoming cars. If it means catching an earlier train, getting on line for coffee, or just getting to the other side of the street before everyone else, they're willing to chance it.

The traffic in New York is also more extreme. It's actually out of hand in some areas. I lived in Brooklyn for a while, on a busy block near where the Barclays Center is now located. Jay-Z fans will recognize my address as his former stash spot: 560 State Street. Jay-Z and I didn't hang out. If we had, I'd probably know what a stash spot is. But in an entirely nonsimultaneous sense, Mr. Carter and I both lived on one of the busiest and loudest corners in Brooklyn, at the intersection of Fourth, Flatbush, and Atlantic Avenues. The whole time I lived there, it was under construction. Poor Andrew Sullivan would have needed acoustic wall blankets.

The intersection was exceptional, honestly, even for New York. Nobody *ever* crossed against the light. There was no point in testing your urban mettle, because you'd get plowed over by a cement mixer. A few years after I left that place, I read that the transportation department had decided to fix the pedestrian crossing there. A local paper reported—with no irony whatsoever—that the walk sign would flash for *thirty-one seconds* instead of its previous time of *eight seconds*. Eight. Fucking. Seconds. That is literally—and I know this because I ran a stopwatch—the amount of time it's taken you to read this sentence. The best part was how local officials justified the fix. The rationale behind the new walk sign was reportedly to *give pedestrians a chance to move across the street without oncoming traffic moving at the same time.*

Transcending your judgmental attitudes may require you to acknowledge that your own belief system is wrong. And I had to think about that. I had spent more than twenty years living in big urban areas, and I'd gotten used to fighting—sometimes literally—the traffic. In New York, for example, I once had a minor tussle with a cab driver. I was skating home on Rollerblades when a taxi cab made an aggressive right turn. There were no orange flags on Second Avenue, so instead, I skated a block down to the next intersection, where he was stopped at a red light, and spit on his car. He was pretty mad. Especially because, as it turned out, his window had been open so I didn't actually spit on his car so much as I spit *on him.*

I don't know where I learned that classy move. Probably finishing school. But eventually, here in the Midwest, I realized I needed to address my aggressive attitude. Just because someone uses a flag to cross a street that isn't busy, one block from a stoplight, when they are a grown-ass adult, doesn't mean they've entirely lost the evolutionary race. Frankly, if you move to a small town in the Midwest, you bowed out of that race a long time ago. So really, who cares? I can't condone flag-assisted walking, and I'll certainly never do it myself. At the same time, there's a line between militant pedestrians and stark-raving-mad ones. Spitting is definitely on the wrong side of that line. As much as I hated to admit it, orange safety flags probably weren't.

2. I CAN'T SEE SHIT!

It's a cliché to say New York is the city that never sleeps. But the fact is that while the rest of America is wearing orange glasses at night to filter the blue light on their mobile devices, New Yorkers have to set their circadian clocks to a 24/7 light show. Times Square probably uses more electricity in a single day than a small Eastern European country does in a year. Live there long enough, and the electric dazzle fades into the background, along with the man-spunk smell of ginkgo trees and the boxes of kittens in the subway being "cared for" by a homeless man. In other words, you get used it.

Some people get sick of city lights, though. Several months after we moved to Wisconsin, I met a couple named "James" and

"Kaia" who had just left Chicago. They had a newborn baby and were not yet gainfully employed. I asked them to tell me why they'd left, without even having jobs. James said: "Everyone on our block had been mugged, and we didn't want to be next." Kaia said this: "There are no stars in Chicago. Like, ever."

In contrast to the city, our little hamlet in Wisconsin is roughly as well-lit as Mirkwood, the fictional forest from *The Hobbit*. There are no giant carnivorous spiders here, to my knowledge, but I can't say for sure, because it's hella dark. Sometime before we arrived, the town elders apparently passed a law that restricted outdoor wattage. *Mmmmmkayyyyy*. I don't know how bright it was before we got here, but we found this new law against porch lamps extremely confusing. Prior to the relocation and that transitional month in the cornfield, all we knew about wattage issues was that we'd 1) get a house, 2) get light fixtures, and 3) put lightbulbs in them. Then one day, while visiting town hall to pay a parking ticket, someone handed me a pamphlet about "compliant fixtures" and explained—in a tone of voice that makes me understand why some people hate *Greenpeace*—that we should be sure to respect the "dark-sky ordinance."

I momentarily considered dying. But since I had once met a leftist with a sense of humor, I waited to see if there might be a punch line. Nope, it was a real thing. And not just here, in the forests of Mirkwood. The entire town was getting caught up in a similar brouhaha, and it was unfolding in real time. I wouldn't rule out eventually killing myself, but first I had to catch up on the facts.

In the town proper, it seemed, some folks wanted to put lights along a bike path. Their radical program was that lights would help the environment by encouraging people to ride bikes more, help kids get places on their own, and maybe even protect women from sexual assault. That may sound like crime hysteria to city folk but then again, do you know how many serial killers have actually come from Wisconsin? Stroll down a dark path out here, and your skin could end up on a lamp shade.

The other side responded that the bike path was surrounded by residential homes, and that outdoor lights were a plague brought on by serial killer haters and people who wanted to infringe on the rights of barn owls. Or something like that. When I said I was "catching up on the facts," it was more like glancing at an article that I happened to see in the free newspaper bin at the mini-mart. Just because you're waiting on line to pay for gas doesn't mean it's not research.

Listen, I think owls are cool. Birds of prey, in general, deserve a lot of respect. Mike and I mostly steer clear of them while they're in flight, ever since that one very dark morning when Mike took a walk and an owl—possibly mistaking his towering bedhead for a bird's nest—swooped down and attempted to prey on his hair. It pulled up at the last second, when it discovered that Mike was not, in fact, a tree. But as he said, shakily, when he got back to our house: *You really don't know how big owls are until you are face-to-face with their talons.* So long story short, I was never able to interview an owl about its bike path preferences.

As it turned out, however, some (and possibly all) of the owls in question were actually people who had tagged their movement with the acronym OWL: Outdoors Without Light. That seemed reasonable because . . . wait, what? You encourage grown men with buns to use orange safety flags to cross the street, one block away from a stoplight, but you can't put *safety lights* along a path so innocent children can bike home in the evening without wiping out on a pile of walnut casings, and women can get in their ten thousand steps without worrying their severed heads might end up in some dude's refrigerator? Sure, that makes sense. Fuck little kids and women! *But who will speak for the bros and the owls?*

I'm not lobbying against the owl people or their fake avian mascot here, so cool your tits, Greenpeace. But just because you own a house near a bike path doesn't mean you can endanger the lives of the people who use it. I know it's tough to hear, but civilization involves trade-offs. If you want humans to be outdoors after the sun goes bye-bye, you have to supply them with a mechanism for seeing shit. Which, last time I checked with Thomas Edison, was called a lightbulb. And this brings me back to the DSO, the dark-sky ordinance of Mirkwood, about which I did actual research.

As chapter twenty-two of the ordinance handbook plainly decreed about the "Regulation of Illumination," bright lights on your front porch or back deck cannot "trespass" onto neighboring property. Illumination in a "large city," according to one DSO pamphlet, "brightens the night sky for surrounding communities, changing their rural character and robbing them of the stars." Apparently, all of these lights that conspired together to help big city folks live life after the sun went down were also preventing rural people from *getting quality sleep.* Wow, I thought, mind blown. Although I did have some follow-up questions. One: Did the rural insomniacs ever consider putting up the urban version of the DSO, otherwise known as blackout shades? Also: What was really at the top of the endangered list in our neighborhood—owls or hypersensitive white people?

I know that democracy and private property don't always get along. But if you are perfectly entitled to not vaccinate your children from whooping cough, in my humble opinion, you should be able to use a porch light that allows you to see the meat that's cooking on your grill. When I mentioned this to a friendly neighbor of mine, he told me the DSO was mostly in place to stop "egregious violations." Like, lights on timers or motion detectors that are being "unnecessarily activated." Um, okay, but I have receipts. One of my neighbors was actually confronted about his outdoor bulb wattage. On the sidewalk! By a person he didn't even know! I wasn't taking any chances, lest we get run out of town by an angry coalition of local hippies and amateur astronomers, who somehow believe that this "large city" is infringing on their natural-born right to see Orion's belt whenever the fuck they want to.

I was mad about this issue for like, a minute. Maybe two. It didn't affect us at home much, because, as it turned out, we don't really sit outside. Mike hates bugs and I'm afraid of being rolled by a raccoon. Also, the outdoor grill we had dragged all the way from New York—although it was actually legal here—had a broken ignitor and rather than get it fixed or get a new one, we just didn't use it. But I got a little mad again when the dark-sky dragnet removed the light-emitting bulbs from all the streetlamps. Some bullshit about safety. Streetlights are dangerous, because they cause a glare and prevent your eyes from adapting to the dark? According to their logic, you can't see Jeffrey Dahmer lurking in the shadows ahead of you, and take proper precautions to stop yourself from becoming a human lampshade, because it's too light.

How did I not know—even after living all those years in New York City—that lights were a safety *hazard*? Here in the suburbs, it would seem, creeps don't lurk in the dark waiting for unsuspecting victims like they do in dark alleys or the lobbies of apartment buildings in the city. Here, criminals lurk in the shadows *cast by streetlights.* Once we are liberated from the streetlamps—and free to take a stroll in the pitch-black night— our eyes take on the nocturnal properties of an outdoor cat's. So thank you to the dark-sky dragnet for cleaning up that mystery of evolution! Just don't tell this to the dude who livetraps the outdoor cats or he may come for you next.

Personally, I have come around to the view that the dark-sky law works, though not exactly how it was intended. With no functional streetlights, nobody walks around at night anymore. We're all locked up inside our homes and cars, safe from the suburban menace of being able to see our own hands right in front of our faces. At the same time, the stargazers in neighboring communities are happier because their property—the solar system—has finally been returned to them. And human relations are on the mend, because nobody's floodlights are attempting to sneak across property lines and remind everyone that living in a "large city" isn't supposed to feel like camping.

Over time, I came to accept the owl people and their dark ways. I had to because, really, who has time for this shit? It takes all of my energy just to remember that I have to stop my car every time a college student stumbles off the sidewalk on his way to a football game. So I put this judgment in perspective. They had not yet passed a law requiring us to compost our own poop or bathe in community rain barrels. I do store cans of beans in my basement, but not because it's required by law. I just like chili. And hey, maybe they're right about the dark sky helping us sleep. I wouldn't know, because I'm still a terrible insomniac. But at least now I have an excuse for the fact that I almost never have fun after sundown.

3. WINTER IS THE REALEST SHIT OF ALL!

There's no place more beautiful than Madison in the summertime. It's warm, it's lush, the air is fresh, and while the scary cornfields mostly grow feed corn for farm animals, the sweet corn is pretty delicious. At night, you sit by the fire pit and roast marshmallows while the fireflies draw circles in the air and the bats eat the mosquitoes. It's magical and peaceful and you want it to last forever. Then you blink, rake a fuck ton of leaves, and it's winter.

Every joke that you could possibly make about winters in the Upper Midwest has already been made. It's important to say, I think, that a lot of people here truly love the winter. They loved winter even before climate change turned it into Cold Seattle. For people who move here from less frigid climes, however, Wisconsin winters still feel a bit like taking an extended vacation at a fancy mountain ski resort, but without the mountains or the ski resort or anything that could reasonably be described as fancy.

Some of us hate winter more than others, though. Five years ago, "Marley" followed her husband to the heartland from a "bustling and hip downtown neighborhood" in Portland, Maine. Describing herself as a "crusty New Englander who had grown up on overstuffed couches," Marley was skeptical about relocating to a quiet suburban neighborhood, with all of its "uncomfortable Scandinavian furniture." But like us, they admired the family-friendly atmosphere in Madison, so they looked for the "most quintessential midwestern-style house" they could imagine for themselves.

The architectural design of their new home was characterized by a lot of horizontal lines and a flat roof with a broad overhang. Stylish! Except that in the winter, the overhang was home to two-foot icicles. Sharp as daggers! One day, as her husband was assembling a crib, Marley set her bundled-up little boy outside in the front snowbank to play and lick the snow from his mittens. She went back inside, thinking about how much she liked her new neighbors, and shut the door. At which point, the front window caught a gust of wind, flew open, and "sent a cascade of icicles from the roof into the snow, imprisoning her son in a frozen dungeon." Winter: 1. Marley: 0.

Marley is hardly the only person to experience winter's shock and awe. Remember "Hallie," who lost the coin toss (twice)? She moved to Wisconsin with a one-year-old and within a year had a second baby. When she talks about having to entertain a toddler in blizzards and arctic temperatures, she looks a little bit like someone who just checked in at a fancy ski resort, then got punched in the face. One day, desperate for diversion, she packed up the kids and took them to the mall. She knew she had hit an all-time low when she headed out into a snowstorm to let her kid run around a "germ-infested play space in a shopping mall." As she shuffled across the mall parking lot with two kids in snowsuits and all their gear, she swore she was *done*. That evening, she told her husband that while she had grown to like the Midwest, they were moving to California. Ultimately, that move didn't happen. They started interviewing, and found some potential leads, but by then it was spring. And just like a woman who goes through twenty-four hours of back labor—and then forgets how fucking painful it was and gets pregnant again, *on purpose*—Hallie decided to stay.

Here's one more story about our midwestern winter to illustrate the Judgment phase. When "Hope" moved from her native Florida to Texas, she experienced some culture shock, but it was a "much bigger change to move to the North." Like so many people who relocate by choice, Hope embraced it. Their first Christmas in their new house here in Wisconsin, she and her kids strung lights all over the yard. "We used to string holiday lights on our crape myrtles," she said. Crape myrtles are Texas's state shrub, and they were all over her property in Dallas. In the new northern climate, they decorated pine bushes, like they were making a festive family tribute to Aldo Leopold.

Later that night, however, it snowed. Four feet, to be exact. The pine bushes were completely covered. Hope recalled feeling two different but equally judgmental emotions. First, she couldn't believe that after all that work, they "could not see one fucking holiday light. In fact, we didn't see the fucking lights that whole fucking winter." Second, Hope was pretty sure that her neighbors were laughing at them. There they were, "shivering outside in [their] fleece jackets" while they put up the lights, and nobody had said anything. She felt like they'd all been sitting in their living rooms or driving by in their cars, thinking what "dumbasses those people from the South are."

I suspect the real answer is that Hope's neighbors didn't even notice because they were inside, using lightbulbs. But who knows? In the end, the facts of the case don't matter as much as Hope's feelings. Or Marley's or Hallie's or mine. Because what all of these stories teach us is how normal it is to experience a cultural shift from the Honeymoon phase to the Judgment phase. While long, harsh winters are a problem unique to certain areas of the country, they illustrate a point about culture shock that we must all abide. No matter where you land, you aren't likely to adjust to your new culture in one season. Especially if that season is winter.

4. TARGET

Of all the stuff that made me judgy in the Judgment phase, Target was the worst and longest lasting. Sure, I had an initial love affair with the phenomenon of the suburban Target. I got the coffee, and the storage bins, and the laundry soap. But after a few months of buying shit I didn't need, it all went sour. Not long after that, the zoning people green-lighted the construction of another Target store, only a few miles away from the two that already existed in the area.

I complained about it to anyone who would listen. I wasn't hating on Target, per se. But that new store did happen to represent perfectly the differences between our old lifestyle and our new one. When I lived in New York City, I never went to big-box stores because we lived within walking distance of smaller, locally owned stores. But apparently, while we were doing that, big-box stores were taking over the rest of America, so every American would be guaranteed the right to fill their giant red shopping cart with mass-produced kitchen supplies, crappy plastic belts, eye shadow made from animal carcasses, and a metric fifth of mediocre tequila.

While the greater Madison area hardly typifies the American suburb—it's an unusual and sometimes explosive blend of smart people, old hippies, wealthy conservatives, and college kids— what makes it perfectly representative of suburban America is its citizens' shared love of Target. Except for my mom's best friend, Lynn, from the iced tea squad—who bitches about big-box stores as much as I do—people around here will sooner complain about Whole Foods than Target. And I get that Whole Foods caters to the free-range bourgeoisie who buy microscopic Amazonian nut bars for ten bucks a pop. Regular working people can't afford that nonsense. But when the hippies get on board and slam Whole Foods for trying to sell capitalism with every pair of Toms shoes—No unions? Imposters! Genetically modified foods? Polluters!—I have to return to the subject of Target. Because that's just straight hypocrisy.

If greed is responsible for Whole Foods, what's the main force behind the proliferation of Targets? Please. If that store catered to regular working people, they'd have built the new one on the south side, where Walmart is. Target pushes an upscale cheap chic brand and markets mass consumption to a broad social demographic that includes the capitalist polluters who live in my pitch-black neighborhood. And Target is just as antiunion!

What really bugs me about Target is that it's particularly successful at pretending it's different. By portraying itself as progressive and chic, it moves tons of plastic crap made overseas under unsafe working conditions and shipped across the world.

Branding itself as fresh and hip, it actually smells like a combination of hormone hot dogs, chemically processed polyester clothes, and Febreze. Its toxicity is rivaled only by its ubiquity. It's the environmental equivalent of Halloween costumes for dogs. Just because you find it entertaining to see your designer dog dressed up as French fries doesn't mean that's a good idea.

Periodically, when I was deep in the Judgment phase, I tried making arguments like these to my neighbors. But nobody seemed to care that the big-box superstore invasion might turn this unique little town into a plastic suburban wasteland. Simple does, in fact, have a good side. It's one of the reasons we moved here, and while it's not about orange flags, it's also not about convenience. In this town, you can still buy your meat at the market every week, from the farmer who raised the animal. You know the people who run the neighborhood bars and restaurants. It's accountable capitalism and we like it. After a while, though, I started to sound like a broken record, and I wasn't changing anyone's mind. It was like bragging to them about how Mike and I always go out to dinner and a movie during big sporting events in town because we can get the best seats and service. They didn't get me at all. *Why would you see a movie if you could watch football? Didn't you know we were playing Minnesota?*

Reader, I still avoid Target, but the ranting had to stop. And I will say this: My judgy revolt against shopping at Target was an important step in the evolution of my culture shock. It was a critical part of settling into this new cultural landscape with a clear vision of who I was and why I was here. How would I make peace with the proliferation of Targets? How would Abby get in with the spontaneous playdate crowd? How would people

like Hope and Christopher handle local challenges like holiday
decorating and online dating? The answer to many of these
questions can be found in part three: the Adjustment phase. See
you there. Don't forget your parka, and a flashlight.

PART THREE

Learning to Adapt

Chapter 7

LET THE ADJUSTMENT
GAMES BEGIN!

IF YOU MADE it all the way to part three without chasing away your neighbors or vandalizing a big-box superstore, congratulations on your fortitude and perseverance! I'm familiar with those qualities, because I spent a year in Providence, where a bunch of normal stuff happened, then a woman in a GMC Yukon rear-ended my car and called me the c-word. After that brush with Rhode Island's finest, I decided I could handle anything. And I hope you feel that way, too. Ready to tackle the big middle phase, known as Adjustment? Perfect!

Before we go there, however, let's talk about the word *perfect*. A lot of people use that word nowadays. It sounds positive and perky, like the women who have to yell over obnoxiously loud music to sell makeup at the MAC counter. But *perfect* is an imperfect word. In fact, it's a problematic word. Because real talk, Reader: Nothing in life is perfect.

If I could be granted one wish—besides instant global matriarchy—it would be that you keep this message and hold it close for the remainder of this book, as your spiritual guide and keeper. Because "nothing is perfect" is the perfect antidote to judgment. It also happens to be true. Even if you are pretty

close to having a perfect life, you probably still have split ends
or a loud sneeze or a penchant for lecturing people on their
"neoliberal" politics because you once played a bongo drum in
front of a bank. Hashtag: #getahaircut. Hashtag: #closeyour-
mouth. Hashtag: #neoliberalisadumbfuckingword.

I bring this up now because guess what. Your adjustment
won't be perfect, either. It won't be linear or uniform or even
always move in a single direction. Some things will be easier to
adjust to than others. Some of your judgments will be harder to
shake than others. Don't be surprised if you find things you
love about winter but never get used to living around conservatives. You might learn to like cornfields—in the fall, when
they're turned into mazes for Halloween agritainment—but never
change your mind about raking. My mom always taught us this
and I still believe it: You will succeed as long as you don't let
perfect stand in the way of good.

When "Marley" accidentally imprisoned her son in the icicle
jail, their recovery was slow. She did eventually convince him
to put on snow pants and play outside, but she never became
a fan of the long, cold winters. Meanwhile, "Hallie" pushed
through her winter anger by learning to look forward to spring.
She also told herself that "global warming was making the
winters here less bleak." Perfect!

When I think about the unpredictable nature of adjustment,
I think about noise. Like many city lovers, I'm afraid of the
dark. When we first arrived, I was also afraid of the quiet.
Our first few months in Wisconsin, I was especially spooked
at night. Every time I heard a noise, I'd run to the kitchen and
grab a knife, until I realized it was just a raccoon picking the
lock on our compost bin. When we bought this house, the former

owner said she hadn't locked her front door in forty years. Know what I said? Ha! Ha! Ha! I lock every door. And turn on the alarm system. Even when I'm home. Fuck that—*especially* when I'm home.

Wisconsin has a few noises. Like, there are birds. A few times a week, we can hear the freight train pass through our village on its way to the fracking fields of North Dakota. In the spring, we can hear the tornado siren. It sounds off once a month for practice and—in the event of real emergencies—about five minutes after a tornado has touched down. But when we first moved, I was actually distracted by the quietude. I had to cover up the silence by running a white-noise app set to "city streets."

On its surface, this appears to be a textbook case of the Judgment phase. Right? Well, yes—if the story ended there. But as with many other things I hated, including the ubiquity of Target and the dark-sky dragnet, I had to face my judgy feelings and try to get past them if I was going to live here and have friends. And while I still miss the hustle and bustle of that beautiful Big Apple, I had to be honest with myself: Wisconsin may be a little too quiet, but New York was way too loud.

Noise in New York is an actual scientific problem. Living right next to the subway, for example, can be a certifiable health hazard. Government people periodically have to come out and measure decibel levels to make sure residents don't lose their hearing. Experts tell us that chronic noise can also cause cardiovascular illness, psycho-physiological problems, and changes in social behavior, although in New York, I'm not sure anyone would notice.

New York is also full of people having fun, at all hours of the day and night. That's one thing that makes it so great. In my younger years, my friends and I would climb to the rooftops of our apartment buildings at night, play musical instruments, sing, talk, laugh, and try not to get so stoned that we fell over the edge. I never liked the war zone that was Fourth of July in the city, but the rest of it was background noise. Then I had a kid and I was like, get off my fucking lawn.

When my first daughter was a baby, she only took thirty-three-minute naps. I know this because I sat there every day and timed them, like a crazy person. I met Mayor Michael Bloomberg one day at the Metro Diner on the Upper West Side. I must have looked pretty out of it, because despite being on his way to an annual memorial service for firefighters, he stopped to introduce himself and share some inspirational thoughts. "You know," he said, in his heavily accented, singsongy voice, "eventually, they *all* sleep through the night." Later, after her thirty-three-minute nap, my daughter heard Mayor Bloomberg on public radio. She looked up from her highchair and yelled, "Mumba Bumba!" She obviously found his leadership as inspiring as I did.

Around that time, the city passed some noise-pollution laws. They set up a complaint line so New Yorkers could snitch on each other for doing stuff like jackhammering at two A.M., letting dogs bark all day long, or running ice cream trucks, anytime. I know some people think that attacking Mister Softee trucks is fascist, but personally, I hated those trucks. Those infernal jingles are like the Guantánamo of music. So one hot summer night, after being musically waterboarded for three hours, I was like, *Suck it, soft serve,* and I called the noise police.

New York didn't turn out to be the city of citizen-snitches I had hoped for. It wasn't that easy to complain. Like, I could see the truck from my living room, but the woman on the phone still needed a permit number. While I had the ears of a bat, I didn't have the eyesight of a hawk, and getting the necessary intel would've required me to strap on my newborn, take the elevator down twelve flights, walk four blocks to the Frederick Douglass apartments, and recon-crawl underneath the soft-serve window. I'm a tough woman. But c'mon. I didn't want to get spit on.

I called the noise complaint line one other time. My bedroom window looked down onto the roof of this brownstone where some young hooligans partied at least once a week, late into the night. Really late. I'm talking like, eleven P.M. What on God's green earth were those children even doing up there?

This time, I got transferred to a local precinct.

NYPD: "What is the precise location of the apartment?"

Me: "I don't know. I'm looking at their roof."

NYPD: "Then I can't send a squad car."

Me: "Can't someone just drive up the street and listen for the music?"

NYPD: "No ma'am."

Click.

I was enraged.

Dammit NYPD! People are trying to fucking sleep!

Since the NYPD apparently had more important things to do than arrest people for having fun, I was forced to go rogue. I went out onto our terrace, turned on the hose, and pointed it down at their building. Turns out, the only thing harder than guessing the address of a building from its rooftop—especially when you're sleep-deprived and mentally deranged—is hitting that rooftop from twelve stories up with a weak stream of water in a light breeze. Some of the water got there. I know this because right after I turned it on, the youngsters turned the music up and danced, like the only thing their awesome summer rooftop party needed—besides maybe more Special K and a fresh bowl of salsa—was a sweet sprinkle from an invisible magic cloud.

That story is humiliating, and even worse, now everyone knows our secret family code name for Michael Bloomberg. But I had to give you that background information in order to explain adjustment. How could I curse the silence in Wisconsin when I didn't actually like noise, either?

Then a weird thing happened that gave me some clarity and boosted my self-awareness. One morning, before the rain forest of Madison started squawking, I heard a loud airplane. It was, like, right on top of my house. Since Mike was traveling for work and I couldn't wake him up to investigate, I got freaked out. It also disturbed me, I think, because I had a flying phobia at the time. According to my aviation therapist, even the sound of an airplane can trigger the phobia. *Aviation therapist* sounds corny, and please know that I would have continued to ignore this problem—as I do with bunions, because I refuse to trade in my high heels for those flat orthopedic shoes that look like monkey feet—but Mike said that "deformed feet and no travel" was not a good formula for happiness. He also felt that, just as agoraphobics can become prisoners in their homes, my flying fears were threatening to make him a prisoner in the state of Wisconsin.

It would also be easy to blame my panicky response to that noisy airplane on New York. In New York, a surprise airplane was never a good thing. One time—several years after 9/11—the

White House scrambled fighter jets over lower Manhattan and people with PTSD evacuated office buildings all over the place. I was right there with them back then. In Wisconsin, I sensed that the airplane circling above my house was just a Red Baron–style propeller plane, but since I couldn't see it, I jumped to the next, most obvious conclusion. I decided it must be a terrorist and ran to get my knife.

Sitting there in my living room with that high-end chef's knife, as I had so many times before during the raccoon attacks, I thought back to a time—right after 9/11—when I had flown to Memphis for a conference. The taxi driver who picked me up at the airport was telling me about the local sites and pointed out a hotel that, he said, was having trouble booking all its rooms. Because of the recent attacks, travelers were afraid to stay on the top floor. The hotel was *maybe six stories high*. Believe it or not, Reader, the Memphis Holiday Inn was spared.

Thinking back, I realized then that my response to noise was actually a weird, complicated hybrid of my New York past and my Wisconsin present. I wasn't entirely used to the quietude of our neighborhood. But I liked it. I liked it so much, in fact, that I had already become used to birds being the loudest thing in town and started acting like one of those old suburban gals who thought they had to stay alert because political violence in America is *everywhere*. Well, it's not *everywhere*. It's in a few places, including New York. But none of those places is above my house in Wisconsin. The scariest thing to happen in Wisconsin would be a beady-eyed local dude with an NRA membership, faux-military clothes, and a sick passion for playing *Call of Duty*. For real, I worry about that dude every day. Foreign terrorists, not so much.

That's how adjustment is unpredictable. It's a fickle, emotional cluster bomb that explodes all over the place in real time because you are busy living your life as an imperfect human. You may *think* you are a loud urban chick who hates the sound of silence and misses the hustle and bustle. Then one day—at the crack of dawn, with no warning whatsoever—the Department of Natural Resources sends out a big mean airplane to terrorize the neighborhood for the Gypsy Moth Suppression Program and you realize that you do miss the hustle but not so much the bustle.

I had no idea what a gypsy moth was, or why it had to be suppressed, and I still don't, but—because I hate losing sleep, wherever I am—I was enraged. *Dammit, gypsy moth suppressors! People are trying to fucking sleep!*

GETTING OVER YOURSELF

Adjustment doesn't just appear like gypsy moth pesticide. Typically, you have to make active choices, find reasonable compromises, and put in some conscientious effort to get there. To paraphrase the immortal words from *The Shawshank Redemption*: Get busy living or get busy living in Wisconsin.

According to Urban Dictionary—which translates hip-hop lingo for white people and nasty sex things for old people—getting over yourself means to stop being conceited. As a snobby former New Yorker, I can relate to this. I lived in an awesome city. I met different kinds of people every day. Once, my daughter gave Michael Bloomberg a hilarious secret nickname and changed our lives forever. Now I am terrorized by pesticide planes. Sometimes when I go to a coffee shop to write, the people next to me are talking to each other about the Bible. When I go to swim meets, parents are in the bleachers, knitting. I'm always amazed at how well they can multitask while they yell at their kids to swim faster.

Part of moving your adjustment along, though, is directly confronting your judgmental feelings. Examine the culture around you and take notice of how you respond to it. I asked "Hilde" if she had any adjustment challenges in Alabama. At first she did, she said. It was about the local religious customs. Most people she met in Alabama were "fundamental in their faith." One day, after a new friend had invited her multiple times, Hilde went to a prayer group. When the prayer ladies learned of her beliefs about heaven and hell, they backed her into a corner and screamed at her. I didn't ask Hilde what those beliefs were, but I'm pretty sure she didn't deserve the holy bum-rush.

"Clearly I had pushed a button," Hilde told me. She decided she would not be attending prayer group again. It would have been easy, in that moment, for Hilde to ditch those friends and join up with Wicca. Nope—Hilde stepped back and gave it some thought, ultimately deciding that she could avoid the activity but keep the friends. "Oh well," she said cheerfully. "Can't beat the weather!" She focused on what she liked, decided she could live with what she didn't, and got right over herself.

Hilde's compromising attitude strikes me as very practical. Because if you want to make friends, get groceries, and get your kid back into his snow pants so you get a minute alone indoors to poop by yourself, it helps to remember that moving is a *process*, not an *event*. It isn't over in a single round. If you can stop obsessing about the myriad ways you feel you've been cast in a bad modern remake of *Green Acres*, you can make it work. As Yoda once said, *There is no try. There is do. Or do not.* Or maybe that was Oprah. Either way, you really have no choice. You already sold your apartment to that single mom with the MBA and now she's enjoying your brand-new windows and you can never get an energy-saving tax cut again.

In the remainder of this chapter, I will help you reframe communication-specific examples of culture shock in practical, adjustment-oriented ways.

I. TURN DOWN FOR WHAT?

One of the hardest things about moving is not fitting in. This is about you, but it's also about them. Our first year in Wisconsin, we were scrambling to understand what people were even talking about when they strung together random words like *smallmouth bass catch and release northern region season.* Having to learn a new language reinforces that you're an outsider. It also became apparent during that first year that my friends from New York were never going to visit. One or two of them might pass through, once every few years, on a work trip. But over time, I had to accept that if I wanted visitors, I should have moved to New Mexico. People *love* green chilies and hot-air balloons. Icy rain and mosquitoes, not so much.

I was also sad because in New York, being sad felt much more normal. Weeping on the Q train because New York is the best city on earth just means you have a soul. But weeping at Target in front of a woman who is there to buy weed killer and enjoy a venti caramel latte is just coastal white girl nonsense. It's a common misperception that midwestern people, simply because they're nice, want you to share your feelings. If you want to make friends, you have to keep some of it to yourself. And by some of it, I mean pretty much all of it. Why? Because compared to that Target mom, you are a bigmouth bass who needs to be released back into the city. Oh sure, you're friendly enough. But your personality is *a lot.*

I was also sad because I was still judging everything around me and finding it mostly deficient. After raking, then cleaning up dead birds, then getting used to pedestrian supremacy, I still sometimes wondered if I'd made a terrible mistake. Maybe we shouldn't have moved. Maybe I had chosen the wrong place. Had I been wrong to force my husband to live in the climactic equivalent of southern Canada in exchange for quiet evening walks in the pitch dark that we never took? I told everyone I knew—including my parents, our preschool teachers, and the guy who came to install our cable service—that we should probably move back. For a while, it was all I could talk about. Guess what happened then.

Everyone found me incredibly irritating.

I mean, they smiled. They patiently nodded. Of course they did! Midwestern people basically smile and nod in response to every subject, with the possible exception of a negative comment about hockey or pie. Fact is, you have to pick up on behavioral signals like these so you don't make too many mistakes and/or enemies. You know how people like to joke about things being TMI—*too much information?* Like, TMI: I'm sweaty? It took me several months to realize that in the Midwest, pretty much everything—beyond a polite greeting and the possible disclosure of your surname—is TMI.

Midwesterners aren't the only people who don't appreciate your shade. No matter where you move, the people who live there will be annoyed to hear about how great other places are—even if it happens to be true. That's why nobody enjoys other people's vacation photos, even the ones their Russian "friends" put on Facebook. People want to feel good about where they are, even if they did mostly return to that place to die. Most Americans don't want to be reminded every day about how normal they are. They want to be reminded of it twice a year, when they watch the Super Bowl and the Academy Awards. The rest of the time, they want to make quilts, grill meat, and sit in rowboats anchored down with ice cold cases of Hamm's.

Remember how I got judgy because almost nobody understood the word *stoop*? Or really, any Yiddish word that came out of my mouth? Looking back, I had to wonder if some of those people weren't actually just put off by my maudlin displays of emotion. Really, former New Yorker? The Brooklyn Bridge is *insanely* beautiful? The sidewalks near Grand Central Terminal are made of granite? Did you ever *weep* there, Stella Adler? Do you want to say more about the *divine* bruschetta you once stumbled across at the MoMA café, or can I get back to setting up your cable box?

The fact is, Reader, a lot of the new people in your life won't share your views, or your communication style. They may be shocked that you voted for the *female* candidate for president, simply because she was more qualified. They may find you rather straightforward, especially for a woman. They may find your children needy because they want to play. They may scream at you at a prayer group because you have mysteriously heretical beliefs about earning your ticket to heaven.

And frankly, they just might not share your opinion of your beloved city. I've met a lot of people here who have never been to New York. Yes, they know about *The Little Mermaid* on Broadway, and they are fans of the Statue of Liberty. They just don't need to go there. Or maybe they have been there. For a conference. They tried fish, walked around, and they were like: Hmmm. Crowded. No thanks.

As self-centered as I am, I know I'm not the only person who's felt like an outsider. When "Frank" moved from East Tennessee to Washington, D.C., for a new job in the airline industry, he couldn't believe "how much space [he] took up." In the country, people move slower. They aren't in a constant rush. In the city, if he didn't move away from the coffee stand right when he was finished, he felt like he was blocking people. He could feel them standing there, thinking: "Step aside so people can get cream and sugar!" Or if he stood on the escalator: "Move to the right so people can walk on the left!" Frank eventually got used to city living. But in many ways, he still prefers the slower-paced life.

Some Wisconsin natives would humor me while I waxed nostalgic for the big city. Most of these people were elderly and had nothing else to do. "Wow," they'd say, "that must be a big change." Yes, I would tell them, pausing as they turned up their hearing aids, things are very different here. Folks have garbage disposals. They describe things as neat, even when they aren't. New York, on the other hand, is the financial capital of the country. It's one of the most linguistically diverse places in the world. It has roughly 800 different spoken languages, at least 650 of which include the word *motherfucker*.

Making real friends—who actually want to hear your self-indulgent stories and see your travel photos—takes time. I don't think it's a coincidence that a vast majority of my close friends here also moved from other places and are *also* public overdisclosers. Take "Lina," for instance, who moved here from Chicago to work at the local medical school. One time, Lina told me, at a meeting about the recruitment of a junior level cardiologist, she offered to be his research mentor. Then she quipped—because the candidate was male and she is an outspoken feminist—that they'd "probably hire him with a bigger salary than [her] own." Not only did nobody laugh, Lina said, but "you could've heard a pin drop in that conference room." Awkward!

Reader, it helps to understand your audience. I'm not telling you to talk less and smile more. That's a line from *Hamilton*; as a strategy for life, it hasn't really worked out for anyone. Especially women. Still, if you want some of these people to be your friends, you'll have to communicate in a way that will help the locals understand you. Turn it down for *them*, and by extension, for *you*.

Once I accepted that my communication style could be off-putting, even to people who have emotions, I felt more comfortable in new situations. Now, for example, if I'm in a public place and feel like I'm going to cry, I just point my face toward a drunk person. Nine times out of ten, there's one nearby, and they assume I'm just upset about the Green Bay Packers. And here's a bonus cautionary tale: If you ever run out of gas in a small midwestern town, don't ever use the words *panic attack*. Don't pull out your bottle of Xanax. And definitely don't ask an old

German farmer if you can use his phone to call your therapist. All he will hear is your crazy eyes.

2. NO WHINING.

A very close cousin to excessive sharing is complaining. One Halloween, for example, my sister, Caroline, invited me and the kids to come visit her in their very small town, which is so deep in Wisconsin red country that I can't even. On this occasion, however, I did. She brought us to a party, and when we arrived, the kids immediately ran outside. I thought they were going for a hayride. It turned out they were looking at a dead deer. And why not? Going to a party with hayrides is the entire point of Halloween, but going to a party with fresh roadkill in the backyard is the entire point of rural Wisconsin.

The hostess was one of Caroline's colleagues, and I didn't know anyone. So I walked into the living room, opened a beer, and drank it while I looked at some art on the wall. The fact that there was no art on the wall may have made this performance less believable, if anyone had even noticed me, which they definitely had not. Then I walked into the kitchen, where I managed to strike up a conversation with another guest. I wanted to respect her privacy, but it couldn't be helped. The woman was stationed next to a large dish of seven-layer Mexican party dip, which, in my opinion, is the entire point of life.

I introduced myself as Caroline's sister, which didn't seem to impress her one way or another. She also told me her name, which I can no longer remember, so I will just call her "the nurse." I could already tell she wasn't going to be a big talker, which made our close proximity immediately awkward, because I had no intention of standing down from that party dip. To be polite—and mostly to distract her from the dip so there'd be more for me—I started to offer personal information. I was staying with my sister for the weekend. We had recently relocated back to Wisconsin from New York. My kids had never seen a dead deer before. Is it bloody? Is it decapitated? Will it freak them out? Is it better or worse than a cornfield?

The nurse didn't know the answers. To anything. She also didn't leave, which was interesting. She may have assumed that if she left, I'd have eaten all the party dip. And she'd have been correct about that. Out of nowhere, possibly to be nice or break the awkward lingering silence, she asked me a question. What did I do for a living?

That question spiked my baseline neurosis to an uncomfortably elevated level. Technically speaking, I'm a stay-at-home mother *and* a writer. But both of those answers, when presented to total strangers who work outside of the home full-time, can be difficult to explain. Tell them you're a stay-at-home mom and they look at you like you're brain-dead. The fact that I've made mac-and-cheese out of a box about a thousand times and still have to read the directions, *every single time*, doesn't do me any favors on that score. Tell them you are a writer and it's maybe worse, because *writer* sounds simultaneously vague and pretentious, and possibly because of that, it inevitably leads to questions about productivity and achievement that most fragile writer egos can't handle. And that's exactly what happened.

"Oh," said the nurse, chomping on a chip. "So did you write either *The Hunger Games* or *Fifty Shades of Grey*?"

I scanned the table for another snack option. Unfortunately, there was only a plate of crudités, some hummus, and a bowl of pork fried rice. Out of the corner of my eye, I spotted a woman with a Crock-Pot of sloppy joes, and this gave me some hope, until I realized she was just plugging it in. Even I couldn't pretend to like ground meat in cold ketchup. I was stuck.

I took a Hail Mary approach, and just started throwing shit out like Aaron Rodgers in a fourth quarter nailbiter. Uh nope, I explained, I don't write fiction. Actually, I'm not a novelist. I write for some local papers. And, um, narrative essays? I submit work like, to contests and stuff. Like I said, I used to live in New York. So I blog about that. It's supposed to be funny. It's about my adjustment—you know, about moving to Wisconsin and bagging up dead deer and stuff. Ha! Ha! Chewing. Awkward silence. Some actual nail biting. More chewing.

You know that feeling when you are physically still talking, but inside your head, you are in rapid conversational retreat? That was me, and really, could you blame me? Even if you are not a neurotic person living in the land of compulsory smiling, there is just no good way to explain why you've failed to write two of the bestselling works of fiction published in the past decade. I had nothing. At which point, the nurse stepped in to double bag the carcass.

"Well," she said, looking at me with the telltale dead shark eyes. "Maybe you should've thought of doing a book like those."

Reader, I've gotten a lot of sharp criticism over the years. I think I am pretty good at taking it, too. One reason is that I'm female, and live in a patriarchal society. Another reason is that with the exception of a few postpartum years in my midthirties,

I've always been flat-chested. And let me tell you: Nothing builds resilience like growing up in a society that describes small breasts as *flat*. But also, I'm a writer.

Editors—much like midwesterners who give zero fucks about your feelings—are in the actual business of striking right at the heart of why you are a babbling idiot. My own rejection binder is full of fun examples:

"This essay was all smiles and no laughs."

"I wish the meaning of some of these words, or all of them, was more clear."

"Your voice crackles in this essay, but it doesn't slay."

"I would not even have given this woman a PhD."

Two of those comments were from *McSweeney's*. All of them were from men. For a long time, I suspected the patriarchy was just trying to keep me down. Until I met that nurse. Her shit crackled *and* slayed.

I know so many people who have experienced a communication breakdown just like mine. Remember poor "Abby," who got the cold shoulder from her neighbors because of her free-range kids? She's a big traveler and loves to do funky vacations, like snowshoeing to a yurt. After moving to the suburbs of Denver, she told me she soon started to edit herself. She was interested in attending Burning Man, for example, just for the experience. Her husband was fine with it, but he also suggested she might not want to mention it around the neighborhood. She didn't know *for sure* that the Pilates squad hated psychotropic survival festivals full of dirty naked hippies. "When you are new," Abby said, "you just aren't sure how things will go over."

My advice is, keep most of the complaining to yourself until you make real friends. Just as the cable guy doesn't want to hear about your favorite museum, some hardworking nurse in the rural part of a red state possibly doesn't give a shit about your solipsistic blog. People don't move to Wisconsin to hear coastal elites whine about their feelings. They move here for the smallmouth bass.

Sidebar: There is *one* thing folks around here do freely complain about. They *hate* hot weather.

3. SARCASM ISN'T FOR STRANGERS.

While you are busy working on your whining, here's another habit to break: sarcasm. If the strangers don't get your complaining, they definitely won't get your *ironic* complaining. I know this because when I first got here, my sarcasm was out of control. I tried not to offend people within the first few minutes of meeting them, but when I feel stressed or anxious, my default gear is snarky. New Yorkers make snide remarks about shit as a matter of course, and midwesterners really don't. Much to my surprise, they also didn't find the name Crock-Pot particularly hilarious, nor did they understand why you'd even joke about it. Slow cookers prepare meat. While you're at work. How is that funny.

I tend to blame New York for my direct personality, but it's also my parents' fault. When I was a kid, my parents' friends called me Mae West because I made sassy and outrageous statements. I also had a big, talkative family. Growing up with two verbose parents and three siblings, a lot of our dinner conversations were like battles to the death. You fired your comments across the table quickly without the slightest hesitation, because a brief interruption of your monologue might mean you'd never regain the floor. One year, my parents decided to switch things up and turn dinnertime into poetry hour. They thought discussing poems as a family, at dinner, would bring us closer. You know how sometimes you don't even *see* how great a time you had until you look back on it later? Well, poetry hour was not one of those times. But I have to give my parents credit for getting a bunch of angry kids together once a week to read poetry to each other, really fast. They basically invented the poetry slam.

We've talked about stereotypes already, and you can't just generalize the way people behave in big cities, either. By some accounts, you'd think New Yorkers walk around all day bitching at each other for no reason. That's ridiculous, because they have plenty of reasons. Like people who wedge themselves into crowded trains at rush hour with huge, dilapidated boxes tied up with twine. Or the sticky liquid that leaks out of trash bags when homeless people drag them down the street. Or hipsters who slow-walk up the subway steps while staring at their cellphones. Or tourists who stop in the middle of the sidewalk because they're having trouble figuring out where they are in a city that's laid out in an ascending grid pattern, according to an ordinal number system.

It's not like midwesterners lack the gift of snark. They're just more polite and soft-spoken in public. People here put a premium on being *nice*, which, between 65 and 98 percent of the time means passive-aggressive. Remember that woman "Laura" who moved to Los Angeles and got twitchy when everyone moved so slowly? She also spent several years in the Midwest. When she lived here, she told me, it took her a while to figure out that people don't always say what they really think. In a big city, she said, someone will tell you if the wedding dress you're trying on doesn't look good on you, "not to be mean but to be helpful." Besides, if you're in a foul mood in New York and you get snippy with someone, you'll probably never see that dick again. You can't count on brutal honesty in a small midwestern town. People are hesitant to say what they really think around people they'll see again tomorrow at Home Depot. Especially because that person will probably turn out to be your children's art teacher or the head of human resources at your husband's company. You better hope you didn't just call him a dick out loud.

According to "Hanna," a California woman who moved to Wisconsin, midwesterners deal especially poorly with dark humor—not because they don't get it but because their need to help you supersedes their desire to laugh. I asked her for an example. One time when hanging out with a group of new neighborhood friends, she said that her boys were driving her crazy and added something like, "I'm thinking of checking myself into an institution." One of the women very earnestly reached over, touched her arm, and said, "Don't worry, the YMCA has some great programs for kids." It made her feel even worse, because now she was crazy *and* misunderstood. Hanna was relieved when she later met a fellow California transplant, who invited her for dinner. Before leaving that night, Hanna remarked that she had to go before her rowdy son put his head through a window. "Don't worry," the host deadpanned. "It's double-paned glass."

Being snarky in a reserved public culture means, much like Abby said, that you sometimes go too far. That can be confusing for everyone. Our first year back here, I went to a downtown pizzeria during the lunchtime rush and the young guy behind the counter told me—in a slightly elevated tone of voice, which signaled to me that he might be having a negative emotion— that our order was delayed. After checking that my kids weren't sucking on the salt shakers, I walked back to find our slices on a table out in the dining area, surrounded by a crowd of people. The pizza guy goes, "Your slices are out there." And I said, "Over here, on the swine flu table?"

I was totally kidding. I didn't think it was very funny, but I *am* a hypochondriac. And we *were* in the middle of a swine flu outbreak. And *every single person* standing by the pizza was sniffling with the exception of one, who was virtually coughing up blood. So I was venting some anxiety without officially complaining and I was definitely going to eat it! Not a big deal, except that the pizza guy looked shocked or stunned or something, like a cab driver who just got spit on by some crazy roller derby bitch. And like Hanna, I felt even worse, because now I was a weird hypochondriac *and* mean. I went back to my seat and ate my swine flu pizza like a nice midwesterner.

It took a few years before someone told me the truth. It was after school, and I was walking down the hall with my kid's teacher. She was the blondest, trimmest, most prototypical kindergarten teacher you can imagine. I always made sure to act *extra nice* around her, because kindergarten teachers are like sweeter versions of moms who also know how to teach reading. On this particular day, we were talking about upcoming summer plans, and I expressed how psyched I was that school was almost over. She turned to me and asked me to remove my sunglasses.

"I can't tell if you're being serious or sarcastic," she said, "unless I can see your eyes."

Oh my fucking God, I thought, but definitely didn't say out loud. I've been trying to make a good impression on the kindergarten teacher, and all this time she can't tell if I'm serious or joking without *reading my eyes*? Perhaps it was time to make some adjustments.

4. NEVER DROP THE F-BOMB.

Admittedly, I'd never heard the term *f-bomb* until I moved here. I'm sure New Yorkers also say "f-bomb," but only in polite company or because they are legally restrained by a labor contract. In New York, when people want to say the f-bomb, they usually just say "fuck." It's sometimes a howl of anger, sometimes an exclamation of joy, and sometimes both in the same sentence.

The first time I heard the term *f-bomb*, one of my neighbors— a pediatrician, and the second nicest person I have ever met after that sweet baby kindergarten teacher—was telling me about a terrible work meeting. She was so mad about a new partnership policy, she told me, that she "dropped the f-bomb" right in the meeting. It took me a second. F-bomb? "Wait, you said 'fuck'?" That's when it dawned on me. That word is so unacceptable in public here that if you do accidentally let it slip out, you can only describe it later by likening it to an explosive deadly weapon.

Reader, I'm not telling you to change your entire vocabulary or tone-police your real self out of existence. But when you go somewhere new—whether it's Wisconsin or Papua New Guinea—you sometimes have to adjust your words so people can stand you. People in Wisconsin, especially those *from*

Wisconsin, just don't toss "fuck" into casual conversation with people they don't know simply because it's the best word on the planet. Some people in Wisconsin will proactively avoid hearing it. Once, while having my teeth cleaned, the song "Uptown Funk" came on the radio. "Such a great tune," I said, though it sounded more like *"Sush a gay too."* The dental hygienist responded by telling me that she didn't like it because the lyrics—specifically the part that goes *uptown funk you up*—"sounded too much like another word." I've never been so grateful to have a sharp metal blade underneath my gum line, preventing me from laughing out loud.

People can like or dislike what they want. I'm there to get my teeth cleaned, not talk about how funked up the world is. But people do need a mechanism for conveying anger and displeasure. In Wisconsin, that phrase is *I'm sorry.*

Believe it or not—and they know this even better in Minnesota, because Lutherans—passive-aggression *is* a form of aggression. I was hit with a particularly pissed-off "I'm sorry" one day at our community pool. The pool is a crowded and popular place. That is because for six months of the year, everyone in Wisconsin is dressed up like Sasquatch, pretending to enjoy winter sports. Then suddenly, the pool opens, the remaining snow melts, and boom—everyone in the neighborhood is standing around in swimsuits, wishing they had done more winter sports. Everyone except for me, that is. I stand around in my underwear—or did one day, totally by accident, when I took off my shorts and suddenly remembered that I hadn't actually *changed into my swimsuit yet.* If my undies hadn't been red—and I hadn't been simultaneously talking to a guy who knew my dad—it might have been less conspicuous. But you know, I'm kind of a loud-mouth and karma is a bitch.

Despite my own sordid behavior, I do love the suburban pool. It's way better than the public pool in Central Park, which is filled with hundreds of overheated people who can't swim and therefore have no problem telling their kids to use it as a toilet. Our suburban pool is maybe cleaner, but it is certainly less crowded, even when you count the people who went to my high school, which is pretty much everyone.

Still, people do have conflicts over available space. One weekend, I left my bag and shoes under a chair and went to get my kids dressed. When I got back, I found that someone had put her towel and handbag on the same chair. I knew who it was. She wasn't in the immediate vicinity, though, and she certainly wasn't sitting there, so I moved her things to the ground and sat down. A few minutes later, the woman—who, thankfully, was not my mom's hairdresser, because that woman also does my hair now—rushed over to tell me to fuck off.

Well, from the look on her face, I definitely thought that's what she was going to say. That's definitely what I would have said. Or I'd have at least gotten up in her face and asked her why she moved my stuff. Did she overtly express anger? Nope. Not her. Not here. She just stood there for a moment, looking mad, then gathered her things and blurted out: "Oh, I'm sorry! I thought I had put my things on that chair." Then she walked away to find another spot. Potty Mouth: 1. Passive-Aggression: 0.

Listen, I'm not a monster who steals pool chairs. If she had told me to fuck off, I would have pointed out that my stuff was there first. I'd have been totally reasonable about it too, because after living here for a while, I have actually adjusted my language. Marley has too, especially after she took a trip back to the East Coast to visit her parents. While there, she went to the store. On the ride home, she cut off a guy who had abruptly changed lanes, so he drove past her, leaned out the window, and called her a "fucking twat"—right in front of her ailing, war-veteran dad and her three-year-old son. Marley had encountered plenty of road rage before. But after living in Wisconsin for a year—where it happens a lot less, unless an Illinois driver is passing through on his way to blight the pristine wilderness up North—she was surprised at how rude it seemed.

"Hope" doesn't miss the road rage, either. She likes that when she takes her kids to school up North, there are "no guns in the back of trucks." In Texas, she said, men brandished their firearms during episodes of road rage. Many a time, Hope remembers, someone pulled out a gun on the highway to threaten another driver. In Wisconsin, not so much. Just as people in Texas are used to seeing trucks with Confederate flags in the back window, people in Wisconsin are used to never honking their horns. Obviously, that would be too direct and aggressive.

Parenthood kind of tempered my worst behavior before we got here. Before I was a mom, I used to narrate my driving with a steady stream of curses and insults. I didn't even notice it, to be honest, until one day when I was driving uptown with my two-year-old daughter and got stuck on Madison Avenue behind a box truck. I laid on the horn and—in a Pavlovian moment that showed me why my daughter would also never go to finishing school—she yelled out from her car seat: "MOVE IT,

PEOPLE!" *I'd better clean up my act,* I thought, *before this gets much worse.*

After that, I dialed down the rage. Instead of calling a bad driver a "fucking twat," I'd say, "You are acting like a jerk!" If my kids weren't around, I'd scream "Douche bag!" at the cyclists in Central Park. To my kids, however, I would explain that those men were making *bad choices.* After I had kids, I stopped calling our upstairs neighbor a "motherfucking asshole" when he dropped his cigarette butts onto our terrace. I would just go outside, collect all the butts into a little baggie, walk upstairs, and shake them out all over his motherfucking doormat.

My finely tuned urban bilingualism still wasn't refined enough for Wisconsin, though. One night, some friends invited us to a benefit—a costumed trivia night—for their kids' private school. There was a table of eighties rock legends, a table of men with lederhosen, a table of mimes, and I forget the rest. But it doesn't matter because during the game, I popped up—after answering exactly one question correctly—and yelled across the room: "SUCK IT, MIMES!" Some people tittered. Most of the crowd just looked uncomfortable. Coincidentally, we aren't friends with those people anymore.

Changing your communication style doesn't mean adopting a new belief system. I still believe that cursing, complaining, and sarcasm are useful tools in an urban dialect. They're like pressure valves. Diversion tactics. Comic relief. "Making it" in a big city requires you to have adequate language for interpersonal aggression, real or perceived. Like when someone tries to poach your cab. Or when you get food poisoning from the funnel cake at a cheap street fair. Or when you get stuck with a used heroin needle when you're fishing your change from a pay phone. That needle thing is an old urban myth, and it never happened to me, but I would certainly have cursed if it had. Because if a serial killer could dispose of a dead body in a kitchen sink and get garbage disposals outlawed—which, actually, is another fantastic old urban myth—then coin returns could absolutely have been opioid delivery systems.

I miss the bantering New York style of communication, but I can live without some of the aggression. And out here in the provinces, you don't need those pressure valves. There isn't as much pressure. You may need to brush off your manners and observe the exotic customs of the suburbs so you'll have more friends, or at least get invited back to some benefit dinners. Politeness and kindness might even be better, in some ways. Because really, do people lie on their deathbeds wishing they had yelled "fucking twat" out a car window at someone's mom a few more times? Or that they had laid around the pool in their underwear more often, telling people to go fuck themselves? Saying it under your breath—or later that evening, to your close friends—isn't a perfect solution. But as my mom would say, because we don't want perfect to be the enemy of the good, it's good enough.

Chapter 8

THE WORLD IS YOUR OYSTER,
BUT IT'S NOT NECESSARILY
YOUR CLAM

Hopefully you now have the power tools to manage some of the language differences between yourself and the residents of your new town. Maybe you even found out what rebar is, and remembered to politely thank the old man at the hardware store for finding you some, rather than raising your arms in victory and screaming: "Yasss queen!" After turning it down—less of the cursing, complaining, or whatever personality trait doesn't translate well to your new culture—you now have to learn to eat like a native.

Remember when "Mandy" had to eat fruit for dinner because Seattle people hate potlucks? Well, "Jamie" experienced a similar food crisis the first time she went out to lunch with some new friends in D.C. and ordered an eggplant parmesan sub. Everyone looked at her like she "was an alien eating a baby's head." When "Hanna" moved from California to the Midwest, it drove her crazy that so few restaurants served brown rice. Hanna told me how she felt whenever a waiter turned down her brown rice request: "I just kept thinking, *But white rice causes diabetes.*"

Is brown rice a left coast yuppie cliché? For sure. Are potlucks unsanitary? Definitely. Does everyone from Buffalo eat eggplant?

Gross, I hope not. But I respect these different viewpoints because regional culinary variation is real. Lots of folks in Wisconsin would build a wall around their towns just to keep the brown rice out. That's not a political metaphor, though it could be. People in the Upper Midwest also eat a lot of game meat and feel no shame about serving old-school dinner rolls made with 100 percent bleached white flour. You *betcha* we do. Also, the next time you visit Wisconsin, don't bother calling for delivery. Because unless you want pizza or a bowl of bland curry, that meal will not come.

Fact is, food is central to culture shock because it's fundamental to our sense of well-being. Even if you are not a control freak like I am, the process of getting used to a new region's foods—and its lack of familiar ones—can make people feel terribly out of place, or even physically sick. You can learn how to discard a deer carcass, when to remove your sunglasses for elementary school teachers, and how to chat up a nurse at a rural get-together to distract her from the seven-layer dip, but what if your favorite thing in the world is grits and you move to North Dakota? What if you spent ten years living on crispy pig ears and you can't find them anywhere on the Florida panhandle? The first time I ate hot chicken in Nashville, it changed me forever. The first time I contracted a foodborne parasite from a bowl of beans in Egypt, I spent the better part of a day sleeping in a Bedouin cave, drinking lukewarm sage tea. I still like beans, but for the rest of my natural-born life, the smell of sage will make me dry heave. Hard pass, but many thanks to that Bedouin for saving my life.

When I say food, I also mean drinks. In recent years, my hometown has become quite a "foodie town," with tons of great restaurants and craft bars. It has always had an ass-kicking farmers' market, and it seems to grow bigger and better every year. With heightened popularity, of course, comes more drama. One of the most popular food carts at the market sells loaves of spicy cheese bread, for example, and some locals get mad because those cheesy loaves didn't sprout straight from the soil like an onion. The other side of the debate, which is my side, goes like this: That spicy cheese bread is *good*, bitches. It's perfect for a hangover. And if you want me to come buy your onions at eight in the morning, you need to stop harassing my high-calorie bread.

Wisconsin is one of the heaviest drinking places in America. When I spoke with "Hallie," the coin-toss physician, she told me she is routinely "shocked and horrified" by how much people here drink compared to other places, and she used to practice in Boston! Mandy told me that while she feels like a lightweight in Wisconsin, back in Seattle she was considered a "full-blown alcoholic." Restaurant employees were always reminding her that she wasn't legally allowed to bring her kids into bars, which is just called "family night" out in Wisconsin. Perhaps the heavy drinking is a northern climate thing, because "Jamie" told me a similar story. She was considered a "nondrinker" in Buffalo, because she could only throw back six vodka cocktails before calling it a night. In northern Virginia, her colleagues would have two drinks and head home. Worse yet, Jamie said, they never once closed a bar down then "stumbled to a twenty-four-hour Greek diner for breakfast."

Most new places can accommodate our food preferences if we look hard enough for the right grocery stores and diners. But adjustment requires some problem solving, too. It's rarely as simple as accepting a new flavor palate or just "getting used to it." It's like, I always roll my eyes when a chatty old man tells me how to get used to winters in Wisconsin: *There's no weather too cold, there are just parkas not warm enough!* Whenever someone says that, I want to push him into a snowbank and run away. Ha! How warm is your parka now, Dad!?

BEWARE THE DAIRY FRIDGE

Here's a story. During our first year in Wisconsin, I thought Mike might be lactose intolerant. Normally, I would take note of my husband's food complaints and then summarily dismiss them. He grew up in a health-conscious California family. They eat wheat germ brownies and call them "dessert." In my considered opinion, people like this can't be expected to appreciate the finer qualities of a cuisine in which the three main food groups are cheese, meat, and fat.

Mike had some occasional tummy trouble in New York. He never treated it, because every time he saw his physician, the old guy would tell him—with a completely straight face—that he should quit his job. Eventually, he did that. But when we moved here, his stomach pains got temporarily worse. When we scrutinized our household diet, we decided that we actually ate healthier here. We ate more fresh vegetables because of the market, and we got all this free-range, grass-fed heritage meat directly from local farmers. My mom did make him a lot more pies. But as Mike liked to say, "I only eat those for *her.*"

Reader, I could write an entire chapter on pie, and maybe I should have. For now, I will supply only this comment: If you hate pie, do not move to Wisconsin. I didn't think about pie for two decades, except for once a year at Thanksgiving, and now

I can't stop eating it. Once, we went up north and stayed in a cabin and a woman made blueberry pie in a Dutch oven over a coal fire and it was so good I almost converted to Amish. You know how people say "Shut your piehole"? That's not a joke here. It's just practical, and directional. Because everyone here knows *exactly* where their piehole is.

In Mike's case, we had to problem solve. Racking our brains, for weeks, we identified *one different thing*. It turned out that Mike had been drinking more milk. Of course he had. This state has an agricultural ambassador called Alice in Dairyland. She's a cross between a storybook character and any of the *Real Housewives*. Local stores sell packages of green-and-yellow cheese curds in homage to the Packers. At the airport, you can purchase blocks of cheddar in the shape of the state of Wisconsin. As I told you in an earlier chapter, facile stereotypes are misguided. But when they're about dairy products in Wisconsin, they are *100 percent accurate*.

In the fifteen years we lived in New York, Mike never bought a carton of milk to go with his afternoon chocolate chip cookie. Coffee in a blue-and-white cup, maybe. A can of imported coconut water, perhaps. A vitamin-infused energy drink that contained trace levels of unregulated horse testosterone, probably. But milk? No way. Not one single time. Where was he drinking milk here? The dairy fridge at work, of course. Always stocked. Ready to guzzle.

I consulted several medical websites about lactose, and they all said the same thing: There's no cure for intolerance; the only way to improve symptoms is to remove milk products from the diet. Curiously, there was one outlier: the Wisconsin Milk Marketing Board. Their website suggested—because you can't make this shit up—that if people were lactose intolerant, they should continue to consume the recommended number of servings of milk and other dairy foods. Their position seemed to be that the way to get better at drinking milk was to drink more milk. It's like playing hockey here, or abusing alcohol—just practice more!

In the end, we cured Mike's stomachache by ignoring the dairy industry. He cut back on the milk shots and felt better. My own story about food adjustment didn't have such a happy ending, although—as with many vexing situations in life, including what parka to buy for the winter—I got some solid advice from my dad.

FOR UNREQUITED LOVERS OF SHELLFISH

Wisconsin has a lot of good food. Milwaukee has kick-ass German food and biker hotels that serve biscuits so buttery, they probably cure lactose intolerance. Wisconsin milk may be pushed on people like opioids, but it is objectively the best milk in this country. And Madison, charming little Madison, balances its big-box store fetish with an eminent farm-to-table restaurant scene that puts many towns this size to shame. Also, fun fact: The Midwest has one of the world's largest supplies of freshwater. That's literally why all the Asian carp are coming here. If I were a rich person from California, I would buy a cabin out here and start hoarding H_2O, stat. Don't say I never warned you.

Freshwater is great. It sustains life and will someday cause Wisconsin to be overrun by thirsty California hipsters with expensive Canadian parkas. But as much as I like freshwater and the trout and whitefish that swim in it, I *love* saltwater shellfish. New York has *so much* shellfish. Not everyone in New York consumes towers of freshly caught raw bar items at lunch, but you *can* do that if you want. And I did, too. Nothing makes me happier than driving to the ocean and picking up a basket of fried clams. One summer, I got invited to a party in East Hampton that I will never forget. They had two garbage-bin-size tubs of fresh oysters, and all day long some chef, who I wasn't yet sophisticated enough to identify, stood there and shucked them. The only thing more incredible than the food was the mason jars full of rolled joints that adorned every picnic table like the world's best amuse-bouche.

Someone right now is calling bullshit. What?! It's possible to get decent shellfish in Wisconsin! There are amazing chefs here, and they get lobster via overnight delivery! That's true. And not everyone in New York pushes their way onto the subway. But we've talked about the partially accurate nature of stereotypes, and, on the weekend of my fortieth birthday, when my friend Tara flew in from New York and we drove up to the Wisconsin Dells for a girls' weekend, at least one of these partially accurate stereotypes was confirmed.

"The Dells," as it's called here, is a tiny town whose main industry is water parks. All summer long, but also in the winter, people drive from neighboring states to toss their kids into the wave pool and drink frozen daiquiris in thirty-ounce cups. While there, you can watch a laser-light show, ride some bumper cars, and catch a waterskiing exhibition. So naturally, Tara and I skipped all of this and went to a spa.

For dinner, our hotel concierge recommended a nearby steak house. Given that it was a Sunday night at the end of the summer, we shouldn't have been surprised that the place was nearly empty. We also weren't very hungry because the night before, we had feasted on gourmet Scandinavian food. Which is an actual thing. So Tara ordered a salad, a side of vegetables, and a baked potato. I also got a salad. Then for some reason— perhaps because I was with my BFF from New York, or because surf and turf is a common pairing at steak houses, or because I wanted to treat myself for my birthday, and because I had already ruled out everything else on the menu—I ordered a plate of clams casino.

When the waitress first set the plate down, Tara remarked that the gal must have put in an order for escargots by mistake. Tara knows fancy stuff about food. She works in the food industry. She also isn't legally blind. The plate in front of me was an *escargot* dish, a plate with several small, round depressions made to hold cooked land snails with French names, and not prototypically equipped to nestle a bunch of large clamshells. Not that there were any clamshells. And since we're on the topic, there were also no clams.

I was prepared to eat the snails, because it was already getting late. But when we peered into the wells of the escargot dish, it became apparent that there weren't any snails, either. There was some melted butter. Some clumps of salt. Some chopped bits of (maybe) garlic. When I dredged the butter holes with my spoon, I found some shreds of . . . something. Snail? Clam? Asian carp? But the quantity of whatever it was didn't make sense, either. Taken together, all of the shreds didn't add up to a single snail, or even half a clam. After looking at it for a few minutes, I honestly thought I might've been served a dirty plate.

I'm not like, a clam expert. But I did learn at least two things during my tour of duty in Rhode Island. One was that women there use the c-word in front of their children and will even say—without recognizing the irony of the situation—"Don't swear in front of my children, you fucking cunt." The other was that I *love* clams casino. The variations are endless. You can make the dish with bacon and pancetta. You can use red or green pepper. Some people use minced onion, while others prefer scallions or shallots. I prefer mine with Tabasco sauce. But even if you fiddle with some of the ingredients—or tinker with the proportions—the clam itself is not a negotiable part of the recipe.

Unfortunately for me, the restaurant manager at the steak house in the Wisconsin Dells did not share this assumption. "Alan" was sent over to talk to me when I complained about my dirty plate. I had already tried talking to the waitress, but she couldn't help me because she didn't have the authority to send things back to the kitchen. "And besides," she said, she had "never seen a clam before." Personally, I found it *a little* hard to believe that this gal had gone her whole life without so much as sipping the chowder at Red Lobster. But at least she was friendly. Alan had a considerably less congenial disposition.

"What's the problem?" he said, dispensing with all of the polite formalities you learn to expect from people you are paying to be nice to you.

"Well," I said, in the nicest midwestern voice I could muster, "I ordered the clams casino. This," I said, pointing down at my dish, "obviously isn't clams casino."

Alan looked down at my plate with an expression of hostile indifference.

"I'm sorry," he said, "but this is how the kitchen makes the dish."

Recall, Reader, that when someone in Wisconsin says "I'm sorry," they are basically telling you to go fuck yourself. That is especially true when they say it in a tone of voice that sounds a lot like "Go fuck yourself." Tara looked confused and, like me, assumed that Alan was mistaken. Even if he hadn't offered to get me a new dish on the grounds that I was the customer, surely he would do so on the grounds that this iteration of clams casino obviously sucked.

"Um, *I'm sorry*," I said, using local vernacular but warming up my New York dialect for possible future deployment. "But there is *no* way the kitchen made this on purpose. This dish looks nothing like clams casino."

Alan stared at me for a moment, ostensibly considering my plea. If he felt any kind of concern about the quality of my clams, I could not discern it. His disdain for me was palpable, however. He was getting angrier and angrier at me for refusing to shut up and drink the salty butter.

"I don't know how it's made in other restaurants," he insisted. "And I don't eat clams." I had to hand it to them for staying on message.

It probably should have occurred to me that whatever Alan had come over to do, it was definitely *not* to problem solve. Since I wasn't yet aware that I was going to have to solve the problem, I clung to the belief that we just weren't communicating properly. Perhaps if I explained it in a slightly different way, I thought— like, more passive-aggressively—Alan would understand.

To avoid an emotional explosion that I had spent months training myself not to have, I decided to stare at his name tag. In all my years of working in food service, and there were many, nothing bugged me more than customers who called me by name tag while criticizing me. I briefly considered doing this to Alan, but then I looked across the table at Tara, who was staring down at her potato, straining to suppress nervous laughter.

"Here's the thing," I maintained, still turning it down for Alan. "Even if you don't eat clams, you cannot deny that there is something wrong with this dish." I pointed down at the coagulating pools of butter. "It doesn't just have *no clams*. There is actually *no food* here. There is *nothing* in this dish to *eat!*" It was an airtight defense. And I didn't even drop an f-bomb.

Alan responded by leaning in toward the table and—in a low throaty growl—spelling out his restaurant's policy on customer dissatisfaction. It wasn't typical of Wisconsin, or anywhere else in the country where people have restaurants.

"We don't take food back to the kitchen," he barked, "just because a customer doesn't like it!"

We saw Alan one more time before we left, shortly after the waitress brought the check. As it turned out, we hadn't been charged for the baked potato. Tara pointed this out to the waitress. She muttered something about the cost of a side salad, Tara asked for clarification, and the waitress disappeared.

After a few minutes, Alan came out to reiterate that he would not take the clams—let's call them "clams"—off the check. Tara said that she wasn't asking for that. She simply wanted to avoid any further disputes, including any issues that might relate to a free or discounted potato. Alan reprimanded her for trying to pay for a potato that wasn't on the check and stormed off.

Ultimately, we decided that he really just didn't want to adjust our bill in any direction, though it was unclear to us why that was our fault.

"Should I have told Alan it was my birthday?" I asked sullenly as we left the restaurant. Tara shook her head and grabbed a breath mint and a business card. She escaped without a concussion, and for that reason, I suspect she looks back on that night as one of the best restaurant experiences of her life.

This was an unusually bad shellfish meal, even for Wisconsin, and our problem-solving skills were not adequate for the task. On the drive back home, we speculated that the restaurant laundered money for Russia, or had fired all of its cooking staff just the previous day, or was going out of business. We talked about it all the way back to Madison, and when we arrived, we recounted the story to my dad.

Some brief background on my dad: He spent the bulk of his childhood on the Jersey Shore, where he used to pluck clams right out of the surf. He spent the rest of his childhood in Tarrytown, just up the Hudson River from New York City. After forty plus years in Wisconsin, he never lost his craving for fresh shellfish. So his shellfish game is strong. And I figured he would sympathize with some sweet overprotective paternal outrage. Instead, he chose—as he so often does with cold weather and parkas—the path of truth.

"Well, in my experience," my dad said, "it's never a good idea to order an East Coast specialty shellfish dish at a steak house in rural Wisconsin."

Mic drop.

I realize, Reader, that we can't all expect to have my dad available, twenty-four-seven, to translate the local culture for us. I'm not going to offer him up, either, because he just got his hip replaced. But if you know someone like my dad—who knows that adjusting to the new food culture means learning about the local food scene, accepting that it's different from the old one, and figuring out how to navigate it—you should consider asking that person.

Or just use your common sense and eat local. You don't move to New York and expect to have an office dairy fridge. You don't move to Austin because you love hot chicken. You don't move to Nashville because you love fish tacos. And you don't move to Wisconsin to eat clams. If you order clams and the waitress says she's never eaten one, consider changing your order. Order the whitefish and wash it down with a bourbon old-fashioned. The world can be your oyster, dear Reader, but if you want an *actual oyster*, travel to an oceanside resort and order one.

FUN QUIZ

To test your own problem-solving skills, take this quiz.

Also, because quizzes are fun!

1. A colleague at your new office asks you out for lunch. You want to try a new farm-to-table restaurant owned by a James Beard Award–winning chef. She says Panera Bread is her favorite restaurant. The best way to respond is:

   a. Inform her that you didn't spend fifteen years refining your palate in New York so you could eat at fast-food chains.

b. Make the same point in a passive-aggressive way by going to Panera, ordering the broccoli cheddar soup in a bread bowl, and sitting down stubbornly until the "waiter" brings it out with an amuse-bouche.

c. Make the same point in a sarcastic way by telling her you vastly prefer the hot dog counter at Target.

d. Smile and agree to her suggestion.

The answer is d. It's not her fault that she likes fast food. In most places in America nowadays, fast food is *winning*. In some areas, corporate chains are virtually the only eating options, and to trick people, they call it *casual dining*. If this new relationship is important to you, the best approach is to be polite and just be happy she didn't suggest Taco Bell, which I call *grade-D-beef dining*.

2. At an office holiday party, a co-worker tells you that he volunteers a lot at his local church. He has been baking a lot of "bars." You follow up with this question:

a. "The fuck is a bar?"

b. "OMG, you go to church?"

c. "Have you ever made GF bars with stevia and poached rhubarb?"

d. "Are you Lutheran or Evangelical Lutheran?"

The answer is d. New acquaintances will sometimes use confusing food words, like *tuna casserole topped with crumbled potato chips*. Which is definitely a thing. So are "bars," which, in the Midwest, are basically just cookies mashed into a pan and baked like brownies. Feel free to laugh about the bars, quietly, later. They'll get the last laugh when they get into heaven and you don't.

3. Your family attends Brat Fest, where you run into your brother-in-law. He is a lifelong midwesterner who once built a canoe with his bare hands. He offers your husband a brat. Your husband responds that he "doesn't like brats." Your brother-in-law looks like he's going to throw up, then informs him that brats are a "way of life" in Wisconsin, not "just a word." Before things get out of hand, you intervene with this comment:
   a. "He's from California. They eat wheat germ brownies there."
   b. "What he meant is, he only likes brats that are brined in prosecco."
   c. "Do they sell walnut burgers here? We're detoxing."
   d. "I'll take his brat. I haven't had breakfast yet!"

The answer is d. Don't fuck with midwestern German people and their brats. Just fucking don't.

4. A neighbor recommended a list of her favorite restaurants. One of them serves Cal-Asian fusion. One serves Peruvian food. One is a farm-to-table spot that serves hipster dishes like pickled ramps. One of them is a sports tavern. The place you try first is:
   a. The brown rice one, because diabetes.
   b. The Peruvian place, because pan flutes.
   c. The pickled ramps one, because farmers.
   d. The tavern, because fried.

The answer is d. The only people who worry about white rice are rich white people. You already hear *a lot* of pan flute music during your spin class at the local Christian gym. Please, hipsters, pickled ramps were over like, yesterday. Go with what the locals do best, which is deep-frying everything. If it gives you a stomachache, just focus on one of the seven televisions and try to figure out what sport they're playing.

5. It's your turn to bring snack to swim team practice. The practice is a half hour and not very strenuous. Which of the following four snacks do you bring?
   a. Apples.
   b. Carrots with ranch dressing.
   c. Low-fat mozzarella cheese sticks.
   d. Rice Krispies bars and fruit punch.

The answer is d. You can try the fruit and low-fat cheese, but nobody will eat it. They might eat the carrots, if there's a high ranch-dressing-to-carrot ratio. Otherwise, keep in mind that in suburban America, children are rewarded for the smallest amount of athletic effort with hundreds of calories of sugar. Go diabetes! (The rich white people are overprivileged and cliché, but on diabetes, they may also be right.)

If you got at least four out of five correct answers, then you are ready to visit public places without scaring polite Scandinavian people. If you didn't, you may have some work to do before you settle anywhere near the Great Lakes.

Chapter 9

ONE STEP FORWARD, AND BACK YOU GO!

IF YOU'VE EVER been on a diet, you might know how it feels to fall off the wagon. Given how much some of us eat (or drink), it might be healthier to fall off an actual wagon than return to our compulsive habits. I'm familiar with the struggle. One glass of wine turns into four. One cookie becomes the entire bag. One tortilla chip becomes a plate of nachos, and nachos need sour cream! Queen, you can eat salad in your coffin.

After your spouse had an identity crisis and shipped you off to a place where bitchy geese roam free, people hate warm weather, and it's a crime to turn on a porch light, you got over yourself and set your mind to adjusting. You stopped glaring at low talkers. You refrained from disclosing your true feelings, or even your full name, to strangers. When you got invited to a party in the exurbs and you saw dead or partially disfigured wildlife, you shrugged your shoulders and choked down a brat, even if the texture of a brat actually reminds you of partially disfigured wildlife. You are doing great. Keep it up!

It's bumpy on that cultural-adjustment wagon, though. You should expect to fall off once in a while, especially when you attempt cultural reentry into the beloved city you left. This chapter guides you through some of the emotions you may encounter upon returning to the mothership. I can't sugarcoat this for you, and I won't. Because sugar isn't even good for you anymore. And the fact is, sometimes when we return, our identity issues return with us. You may feel the trauma of failure and celebrity withdrawal all over again. So as the kids like to say on the Internets: Buckle up, buttercup. Your long strange trip is about to get stranger, and may even—if you're taking a transcontinental train, as I have done—move backward for a few minutes or completely stall for several hours, with no announcement from the conductor whatsoever.

THE PROBLEM OF PAIN

Ideally, you'll have *reverse culture shock*. After living in the suburbs for a while, you may notice how loud the ice cream trucks are, how pushy the rich people are, or how dirty the pigeons are. I had some of that. As much as I hate it when the finches fly into our windows in Wisconsin—which turns out to be a regular thing, but now I send Mike out with the pasta fork—at least they aren't strutting through exploded ketchup packets then licking it off their claws while I'm eating a breakfast sandwich at an outdoor café.

Unfortunately for your adjustment journey, even the horror of laying eyes on those nasty pigeons is unlikely to turn you against your homeland. It's far likelier that—in spite of them, and the urine, and convoys of double jogging strollers, and the manic street guy dragging you for refusing to give him your breakfast sandwich—you will fall in love with this place all over again. Why? The answer is simple: neuroscience.

It's a general axiom of neuroscience that humans have no memory cells for pain. For example, you can see a wasp and remember that you were stung and remember that it felt bad, but you have no actual mechanism by which to recall the painful sensation. How do we know this about the brain? Well, I'm not a neuroscientist but I do read popular science magazines at the dentist. Also, I have children. Specifically, more than one. Anecdotally speaking, I went to the hospital to have a baby, spent hours straining my abdomen to propel a human head from my southern hemisphere, then about a minute later— as soon as the first head stopped drooling and grew teeth—I went back and did it again. If we had neurons for pain, every human mother would have *exactly* one baby, get sloppy drunk, and curl up around a toilet bowl for the rest of her life.

As far as I know, neuroscientists haven't yet studied the synaptic behavior of people who move. But I will let them have that research idea, because I believe the same cognitive principles apply. You left that cool city because for whatever reason, it had become too painful. The bad outweighed the good. It failed to work out. You lost your kid in a bookstore while the security guard stared straight ahead and cracked her gum. Do you think I remember the exact sensation of pain I experienced during that panic attack? No siree. All I've got is a vague recollection of yelling and running down the up escalator thinking, *Why are these dumbasses facing backward?*

So you go back to the city you left, thinking you've made peace with the pedestrian dictatorship and the brats. But the second you step off that plane, the muscle memory kicks in. You fast-walk to baggage claim, cut someone off for a spot in the taxi line, then take the cab straight to the West Village for a fresh bucket of steamers. Making matters worse, the things you never stopped liking seem even better to you, because you also forgot exactly how good they actually were. Free park jazz! Clustered art museums! Human diversity! Amazing handbags! Anderson Cooper getting Jamba Juice! Tiny Spanish nuns in blue habits riding the subway like a flock of penguins! Wait, the bad outweighed the good? *What bad?*

That was me, on my first trip back to New York. It was Sunday morning, and Chinatown's air was already rife with the aroma of fish guts. After visiting the 9/11 Memorial, which was ethereal, I decided to walk uptown for brunch. I passed a clothing store just south of Canal Street, and Alicia Keys's "Empire State of Mind" was blaring out of the open doors. I got misty, then weepy, then worse. *OMG*, I thought. *I am ugly crying on Canal Street and it feels totally normal. Why does it bug people when crappy clothing stores blast their air-conditioning through open doors when it's ninety-five degrees outside? I'm ready to stand in line for a Cronut and everything is perfect!*

Had I channeled my mother, I might have seen this coming. My mother was born and raised in Chicago. In 1971, when I was two years old, my father took a job in Wisconsin and my mom followed. While my dad had at least lived in a New York suburb, my mom's culture shock was *bad*. She didn't understand why people took "Sunday drives," why the only cheese in suffi-cient supply was cheddar, or why the cheddar outnumbered the people. By her own account, she spent much of that first year listening to Carole King's *Tapestry* album—songs like "So Far

Away"—and crying. I'm not sure where I was while all of this weeping was going on. Toddling around by myself, possibly, trying to stay out of the crying lady's way.

Eventually, my mom stopped crying. She grew to love Wisconsin and call it home. The cheese selection grew a lot more diverse over time, too. She made friends, and made them iced tea. But she has never stopped missing Chicago. Every single time we went back when I was a kid, and we went back a lot, it was the same old refrain. We would pass through the outer suburbs on our approach to the city—where the air started to stink like toxic dirt—and my mom would inhale deeply, like she was smelling a rosebush at Versailles. "Ahhhhh," she'd say, exhaling like a twentieth-century meat packing manufacturer who's trying to put a good face on things for Upton Sinclair, "Chicago!"

She loved taking us back to Chicago. She'd drag us to museums, on walks by the lake, and on shopping excursions on Michigan Avenue, in stores that smelled like fancy perfume. And my mom—who is the least snobby person in the world, and believed she was middle class until eighth grade, when a priest instead informed her she was "lower class"—would do this weird urban posturing that never happened farther north. One time, my older brother pointed out the fancy mirrors in the elevator at the Drake Hotel. After the other people stepped off, my mom scolded him and told him not to call things "fancy" out loud. He was six.

Now that I have repeated my mom's urban transition, I think comparing your new life to your old one is just an unavoidable condition. Madison was a much smaller and more provincial place when I was growing up. A few kids in my grade-school class were farmers who milked the cows before they even caught the school bus. Other than farmers and hippies, all our neighbors were either Swedes or Norwegians. *Both* of our immediate neighbors were big, barrel-chested, backyard beer drinkers. Bob was Swedish and Gordy was Norwegian, or maybe it was the other way around.

This town is bigger, more cosmopolitan, and a smidge more diverse now than it was when my mom first moved here. Yeah, I said a *smidge*. But it will never compare to New York—or Chicago—as a metropolis, by any definition. To me, you can't call a place an *urban center* if there are only four gay bars, one of the major thoroughfares is named after a fish hatchery, and on any given day in a light breeze, you can smell cow manure inside the city limits. When you go back to your city from a place like this—no matter how lovely it is—you can't help but notice what you're missing.

So after taking one step forward in terms of cultural adjustment, you might take a few steps back. Without the capacity to relive your pain, your city might even feel perilously "perfect." You'll probably snap out of this after a few days. But only when you are forced to accept that you no longer belong there.

THE PROBLEM OF TOURISM

Nothing makes you homesick like a visit to the old hood. Nine months after we moved, we went back to visit our old apartment building. I wasn't sure if the kids would remember the place—or even Dio, who was like an honorary grandfather to them. Our older daughter wasn't quite four when we left. But when we pulled up in the cab, there he was. And no sooner had we opened our cab door than she ran over and gave Dio a hug. Well, that couldn't have gone worse!

Staying with friends can also make you feel nostalgic. You could make it easier on yourself and stay in a hotel in Times Square and get bedbugs, but the best thing about having formerly lived in New York is having friends who still live there and don't yet have bedbugs. When we went back, we made the nostalgia worse by stopping in at Zabar's, sitting at the crowded counter next to a bunch of cranky but cute old people, and eating a real bagel. My friend Michelle and I walked through Fairway, shoved people out of the way, and laughed about how they had recently found dead baby rats in the bin of bulk olives. Good times.

Depending on your kids' ages, though, they may well remember diddly-squat. That's especially true if you fled the city right after you started breeding. You can tell them how you rocked them in that bucket swing until they fell asleep, how they dropped an entire box of pastries on the ground in front of your local bakery on a chilly autumn morning, and how adorable they used to look picking crocuses in Central Park. You can even frame pictures of these experiences to display in your new home in Wisconsin so your kids remember them in snapshot form. Still, for a little kid, nine months of cohabitation with barn owls and Target stores is basically a lifetime.

Our first return trip was a lot like that Chicago elevator disaster. Every time an ambulance or fire truck rushed past, horns blaring, the kids threw their hands over their ears and I rolled my eyes in urban shame. Real city kids don't even notice sirens from roughly the age of five, when they go partially deaf. My kids also couldn't ride in a taxi. After not quite a year in

Wisconsin, they'd grown accustomed to riding around in booster seats with child safety locks on the doors. Suddenly, they had to get into a cab in which the previous passenger had spilled coffee on the seat and fret about their necks getting snapped by the old-school seat belt in a collision. Just kidding, the seat belts didn't work.

Adding to our sense of displacement, stuff had actually changed. The Triborough Bridge, for example, is now called something else. I don't know what it is—and I've never had to learn the new name because there are still signs everywhere calling it THE FORMER TRIBOROUGH BRIDGE. And we were such hillbillies, we didn't even think to call an Uber. The hardest part, for Mike and me, was when our kids asked to visit the M&M store in Times Square. New Yorkers don't visit places like that. That would require them to go to Times Square. But that's exactly where my kids' suburban friends told them to go. And we did it. Because we didn't belong there anymore.

THE PROBLEM OF FLEECES

If you watched *Seinfeld*, because you're a sentient human being with a brain, you may remember the episode in which Jerry tells George he can't go outside wearing sweatpants. Wearing sweatpants outside, he says, signals to everyone that you've given up. Nowadays, that's an outdated joke. Sweatpants cost like two hundred bucks. In Los Angeles, people wear them out to dinner. But for New Yorkers, athletic clothes—even athleisure clothes—have not yet acquired the status of actual clothes. Whereas if you leave the city and move someplace like Boulder or Ogden,

Utah, the distinction between athletic and actual clothes doesn't really exist.

Don't get me wrong, Patagonia-pants, I think comfort is awesome. I love things that are warm and cozy. I love electric blankets. I like soft kittens. I'm a huge fan of pre-shorn sheep. I'm not opposed to athletic leggings, particularly if they make it appear that my thighs don't touch. And the fleece—oh, the golden fleece—is the highest form of comfort wear. It's easy to pack. Easy to wash. Unbelievably warm. Totally functional. Fleeces are so popular now that they come in approximately seventy thousand colors and in various warmth and wicking levels. Fleeces are so fuzzy, I sometimes think the people wearing them resemble actual sheep. Maybe they want to. I guess we'll never know.

The casual dress code in Wisconsin isn't for everyone. When "Lina" moved here from Chicago, she was horrified to learn that "Badger-wear"—sporty red-and-white clothing that advertises your affiliation with the local college sports teams—appears everywhere, "including fine-dining establishments." "Hope" feels differently about it. Ask her how she feels about moving from Dallas—where women don't go outside without a fresh manicure—and she will tell you that she has fallen in love with it. They *wanted* to live in a more casual environment, and her "inner hippie" is psyched. In recognition of the difference, though, she did have to invent a new term for those occasions when she wears something slightly nicer than yoga pants in public. She calls it "Wisconsin dressy."

I'm trying to be careful, because around here, poking fun at the pervasive culture of casual wear is a great way to get yourself labeled an elitist. When an East Coast transplant recently wrote in to the local paper complaining about people who wore shorts and flip-flops to the theater, readers called them precious, pretentious, and self-righteous. Were these the same folks who got offended by my tirades against Target? Possibly. The right to shop at big-box stores and wear flip-flops to the symphony are economic justice issues for some people. I don't buy it. Local businesses are part of the economy, too. And other audience members—people excited about seeing a great show, regardless of their annual income—get dressed to the nines, like they're going to prom. The whole debate reminded me of all that postelection twaddle about the liberal elite ignoring the forgotten white man. We're elitist because we wear loafers to the theater?

I'm not saying anyone has to care about fashion. You can move to a chilled-out little biking town for the express purpose of never having to use words like *haute couture*. It's easy to live that way here. It's cold as hell. And the postindustrial economy is a verifiable shit show. But in my not-so-humble opinion, some of the anger at "big city" behavior is just cultural resentment, akin to not wanting to learn new identity-based pronouns or have a black woman tell you who to hire. Closed-toe shoes are not a symbol of economic oppression, unless you're a woman in eighteenth-century China.

ADMITTEDLY, I HAVE baggage about my wardrobe, too. When I was growing up in the Midwest, my sense of style was defined by whatever I saw in the window next to Spencer's at the mall. My best looks in junior high included a banana-yellow pantsuit and a textured hemp-colored vest that I paired with Jordache jeans and an oversize rectangular green comb. It had the word

COMB on it in big block letters, and it stuck out of my back pocket like a slice of sheet cake. In college, when I was a full-blown hippie, I wore nothing but cotton frocks from vintage clothing stores. Since I was a feminist, I also stopped shaving my legs. Looking back, hairy legs kept the macho men away, but may have been somewhat less critical to the cause of feminism than I once believed.

It took me a while in New York to figure out how to look less hillbilly, by urban standards. When I look at pictures of myself from those early days in the city, wearing denim overall shorts and gym shoes, I feel cringey. I still shopped at Old Navy, for years, because that's what I could afford. But I changed my aesthetic over the years, got a trench coat, and started carrying a handbag that didn't make me look like a bike messenger. Look, it's not like people don't wear fleeces in the city. That framed picture I mentioned of my daughters picking crocuses in Central Park? They're wearing purple fleeces. It was April. It was chilly. We were out in "nature." But wearing a fleece because it's cold and you're sitting on grass is different from wearing a fleece because it's athletic chic. Isn't a fleece really just the vanilla suburban equivalent of a hoodie? But that's another topic.

Your fashion standards have to change—again—when you move to a place where you spend a lot more time outside, and your every winter coat has to match a sturdy pair of snow boots. You don't hear a lot of people in Wisconsin bitching about the absence of a Prada store while they bike to work in the middle of winter. Also, the soccer field is not the ideal place to wear a Burberry trench. You can bring a high-end handbag, but it might end up rolling into a mud puddle or getting lost under a pile of sweaty pinnies. Just wear the stupid vanilla fleece.

If you move from one suburb to another, the fashion adjustment is easy. "Abby" wears exactly the same thing every day in
suburban Colorado that she wore in suburban Wisconsin. The
fleece is the uniform of choice in outdoorsy towns across America,
and for those of you who embrace that lifestyle, I say: Ride that
fashion trend like Seabiscuit! If you left a bigger city, however,
it might feel odd to wear the same jacket out to dinner that you
just wore to clean out your gutters. Does it make me a liberal
elite to admit that? Maybe. It's true that I've never eaten at
Applebee's. Or the LongHorn Steakhouse by the mall. On the
other hand, my husband took an 80 percent pay cut when we
moved here. I mow my own lawn. I volunteer for the PTO at
the local public school. And we put that flag out on the front
stoop every Memorial Day and Fourth of July because we do
respect veterans. Can't you be a decent human being and still
love a nice trench coat?

I don't know if clothes necessarily reflect who we are, but
in my experience, they definitely reflect who we *no longer* are.
Almost every day for seven years, I watched my husband put on
a suit with a tie, a dress shirt, and a pair of cuff links. When we
first got here, people at Mike's office were encouraged to wear
jeans on Fridays. Then after we lived here for a while, his office
expanded jeans day. To *every* day. My husband has a box full of
unused French cuff links, and *every day is jeans day.*

But even if you spent the better part of your young adult-
hood trying to murder your inner hippie—life hack #1: no
patchouli, ever!—fleece resistance is futile. I started hanging my
fleece on the closet door at night so that I could put it right back
on again in the morning. *Without washing it.* I would see other
women at sporting events, admire their fleeces, and convince

myself I needed more. I'm talking, like, *multiple* fleeces. Had I given up like George on *Seinfeld*? I guess I felt that way, since I'm the one who conjured that scene at the opening of this section. After all those years in the city, I wasn't sure that taking off your pajamas to put on clothes that are just as comfortable as your pajamas really even counts as getting dressed.

My mom wore skirts or dresses and heels—and panty hose, ack!—every day of the workweek. I always thought it had something to do with her age or her generation or her having been schooled by nuns. In retrospect, I wonder if she just couldn't shake her big city self. Cities make you want to rise to the occasions they provide. Nothing screams *I'm a tourist!* in Manhattan like standing still on the corner of Fifth Avenue and Forty-Seventh Street with a fleece and white sneakers. If you really want to seal the deal, put your Disney Store bag down right on the sidewalk, take out a subway map, and turn around a few times in the same spot, while looking up. Don't forget to visit the M&M store.

At the end of the day, the hardest part of going back to that cooler place you left behind is that—whether you cop to it or not—you *are* a tourist now. When you give your phone number to the hostess at a restaurant, you're gonna get the look they give people who have *an unrecognizable area code.* You can waste your breath trying to explain that you used to live here and that this used to be your favorite crappy bistro. She doesn't care how rude she is to you, though. Your handbag sucks and she'll be done with design school by the time you come back, anyway.

You can walk the walk, and try to fit in and act like you own it, but you can't deny that you not only live somewhere else but have started to adapt to it. On our second trip back to New

York in a year, we went out to eat with Mark and Jenni, the friends who introduced us. I ordered the cheese board, which isn't something I would typically remember, except that it was a sort of stereotypically Wisconsin thing to eat. Jenni, who has an infectious laugh and an acerbic wit, caught the right moment.

"You look great, Erin. I'm actually surprised at how fabulous you guys look. We expected you to let yourselves go out there in Wisconsin."

Holy shit, I thought to myself. *She knows about the fleeces?*

EVEN THOUGH WE had experienced the city in only a small dose—with a handful of close friends and zero ice cream truck skirmishes—getting back to Wisconsin still felt like a bad hangover. For several nights after we returned, I sat on the couch at home, flipping channels like a sullen teenager, trying to talk myself out of buyer's remorse. *Why did we come here? Why aren't people more sarcastic? When will we make lifelong friends? And where is my pullover seafoam fleece? It's fucking freezing in this house!*

Reader, give yourself permission to pout. Complain to your heart's content, in private or around those you trust, because complaining is authentic. Grieve for your loss—of your old life and the person you were before you had kids and gave up awesome healthy habits like smoking for breakfast. If you're going to live in your new home, and not go back to your cool city, you will eventually want to get off the couch again. Not because you should feel grateful about stargazing. Or because you swore allegiance to garden club. But because you made this decision, and nothing is perfect, and here you are, and life is—in fact— too short. Scientific fact. Look it up.

There is more adjustment to come, Reader, but it will get easier. You know it will, because the next section is the Mastery phase! You're not simply managing your judgmental feelings anymore. You're not going to renounce all the great stuff that you still love—fancy restaurants, trench coats, a daily dose of hard-biting sarcasm—and start smiling for no reason and wearing Birkenstocks to the ballet. Your relationship with those beloved things may change, but how much it changes will be up to you. You're *driving* the wagon now, big stuff.

PART FOUR

Mastery

Chapter 10

MASTERING THE ART
OF ARTICHOKES

O UR FIRST YEAR in Wisconsin, I planted purple and
white crocuses in my front yard. It was one of my first
forays into gardening, and, thankfully, one of my last. I was
glad I spent four hours digging all those stupid holes, though.
Not because I was proud of my nature skills or needed that
upper back workout, but because every time I saw those flowers,
at the first blush of spring, they reminded me of New York.

Welcome to that place in the program known as the Mastery
phase. Having just visited your old domicile and returned home
to sulk on your new couch, you may not be feeling the mastery.
You may not even feel like you've adjusted particularly well.
You're asking: *Who the f-bomb am I?* What kind of person wears
a fleece every day but refuses to shop at Target? What kind of
person likes taking the dog out to the backyard and chilling
next to St. Francis in her short leopard bathrobe, yet simultaneously feels 100 percent certain that gardening sucks ass? Waiiiiiit
a hot minute—did I just call this place . . . *home?*

Cultural adjustment can be confusing. You like some things,
and you tweak some behaviors, but not all of them. Which of
these behaviors reflects your authentic self? How do you know?

I barely wear my trench coat anymore, for example, and that's fine. But I never walk in the woods by myself, in any kind of coat. We like so many things about the culture here, especially the local population, which is generally well educated but also down-to-earth. But I still find it mildly depressing that even on a busy night, restaurants only have one seating and then everyone goes home to watch sports. Like so many cars in this one-taco town, I sometimes feel like my life is a boring, slow-moving hybrid. And I want more tacos.

Well, don't worry, Reader. If you're like me, then you're exactly where you need to be. You can live *in* your local culture but not be entirely *of* it. The Mastery phase—also called *biculturalism*—is a process of figuring out which aspects of your new culture you want to adopt and which you don't. The process works whether you're a neurotic writer who hates roadkill or a mean nurse who hates bloggers. Once you stop seeing everything in terms of facile stereotypes, stop judging everything according to the standards of your old place, and problem solve ways to deal with differences, you can accept your new culture for what it is and *yourself* for who you are. You can plant crocuses, and enjoy them, and still feel like if you made a horror film mashup of *It* and *Get Out*, the Sunken Place in the Barrens would look exactly like the "heavily wooded" area near your house.

I felt like I was getting closer to the bicultural thing when I could enjoy the community without feeling like I was compromising my core principles. For example, I try to avoid fights at the pool now, but I don't feel compelled to be overly friendly, either. I might wave to someone if I accidentally make eye contact and/or can't avoid them by walking around the pool in the opposite direction. But sometimes I don't want to talk to anyone, so I just pretend I'm by myself in an elevator. Sometimes people look confused, but it works out. I'll see them later at the water ballet show. Similarly, no matter how many coffee baristas in this town cheerfully wish me to "have a great day!" I will never reciprocate. I won't scowl at them. But, "have a great day" is just way too much fucking pressure. Shut up and give me the damn coffee.

Being yourself—and never using the word *perfect*—is really important. If you don't believe me, just ask any gay person married to a straight spouse, or any girl who ever attended middle school. There are people around here who may wish—because of my occasional bursts of bitchiness—that I would move back to New York. That's fine, they're entitled to their negative feelings, too. Unless there is a pressing economic reason, however—or we get a personal invitation from Brearley, with a full scholarship—it's not likely to happen anytime soon. My kids like it here. The schools are good. Mike knows how to use a snowblower now. I've developed strategies for repelling people whose politics I despise. I have found that a yard sign, a set of very visible head-phones, and a dismissive wave solves a lot of problems before they start.

I wish I'd figured out the headphones trick back when a young woman in her early thirties stopped to talk to me while I was working outside one day, probably raking.

"Hi," she said cheerfully. "I used to be friends with the girls who grew up in your house."

I sensed a story coming. Mayberry never forgets.

"Do you still have that hot tub?"

I nodded.

"Oh man, when we had parties in high school, all the girls—and guys—in the neighborhood used to pile in there."

Perhaps I was supposed to be charmed by that story and invite her inside for a commemorative dip. My internal voice, the one I had learned to keep to myself, had a different response. *Oh hell no!*

Instead I just smiled, thanked her for taking the time to stop by, excused myself politely, and then—the second she disappeared around the corner—I threw down my rake, bolted inside, and sold that nasty tub of high school boy secretions to some woman on Craigslist.

As a cultural master, you can appreciate the best qualities of a place while ignoring or shunning the worst. You can politely converse with a youngster in your front yard about how she used to sit in your sex tub, then toss that shit right onto the slag heap. You can commiserate with new friends about the suburban soul murder of shopping at Target but still appreciate the community that you've all chosen because even though they all dress their kids in the same clothes from Target, they're nice people. Political elections may cause some backsliding. Get those headphones ready.

Not for nothing, but some people won't make it. I met a woman from San Francisco who talked constantly about how much she hated the Midwest. She drove two hours to Chicago to get her hair cut, because nobody in town was good enough for her. She refused to buy a proper winter coat—one that's puffy and made of geese—because she was permanently pissed off about the cold. It does suck when your nostril hairs freeze. But newsflash, bitches: Winter always wins. She lasted two years out here in her lame wool overcoat before moving her family back. I hope she's found happiness there. And that her kids don't feel like luggage. I'd call her a liberal snowflake but that analogy obviously doesn't work in this context. Bye, Felicia.

To me, the most important—and challenging—part of making it in the new place is friendship. Making close and lasting friendships is a high-stakes venture, and mistakes will be made. It's like going on a road trip and pulling over at the first truck stop you come across because you aren't sure you'll find another restaurant. The truck stop was fine. You had coffee and filled your stomach with greasy starch. You didn't get food poisoning. But after driving that highway a few more times—you realize that truck stop wasn't your best option, or even a good one. It was just the first place your car got to, and in retrospect, the food sucked.

As "Marley" told me, finding friends can feel like dating. She tried out different people. She went out and did things with friends of friends when they set her up, even if it didn't seem like a perfect match. She spent a few months trying to get close to one woman, in particular, because their children attended the same preschool. And she thought they were developing a bond. But then the woman stopped returning her calls and seemed like she was avoiding Marley at school. One day—after the woman said she was too sick to socialize—Marley saw her out with another mommy friend. Jilted.

As with dating, you have to be patient. Swipe through a bunch of people until a few of them stick. In my case, most of the friendships that stuck were with women who had also resettled from someplace else. Not entirely. I hang with a squad of my fellow townies, because I know them from high school, and we went to a great public high school, and they are great people.

But the rest of my besties are a band of self-conscious exiles, and we bond through memories of our former homes and jokes about feeling displaced. In fact, Marley is one of these people. One of our favorite running gags is to discuss our wardrobe before going out to dinner in the winter when it's like, negative fourteen degrees outside. It allows us to vent our cynicism about the weather and fashion all at once. It goes something like this:

What are you wearing tonight?
Not sure yet. Thinking about a fleece burka.
Cool. I'm wearing a snowmobile suit, with helmet.
Sexy. Dress it up with the wool blanket from your couch.
Maybe we should just eat on my couch. It's way too fucking cold to go outside.
Even better. I'll bring wine.
TTYL.

"Hanna" is another real-life friend of mine. We've spent a lot of time talking about sarcasm and how our respective communication styles sometimes make us feel like foreigners. She recalled being in an outdoor market in Italy once and picking up some fruit to see if it was ripe. Just as she placed her grubby fingers on it, she saw a sign—in English, clearly meant for Americans—that read: DON'T TOUCH THE FRUIT. She'd never have thought of herself as one of those ugly Americans. But when you're in a new place, you don't yet know *what you don't know.* And that's what it felt like here, for a while. Nobody in Wisconsin put up a yard sign that said DON'T SWEAR. God, I wish they had, though. That would have been so fucking hilarious.

I know that "Ruby" could relate to my experience. It took her two to three years to settle into her family's new life in Scottsdale. They chose a condo instead of a house, because they "couldn't transition from apartment life to a house in the suburbs immediately." Ruby also found some of her best friends in Scottsdale, but—like us, in Wisconsin—their closest friends tended to come from other places, like Toronto, Boston, and Atlanta. "We finally felt at home in Scottsdale when we couldn't go home for a Thanksgiving with family," she told me. That wasn't a typo, Reader. She used the word *home* twice. Deep down, she still felt like a New Yorker, but in terms of cultural mastery, she was solidly embedded in the new place. They filled their house with their "new Scottsdale family." It was one of her favorite holidays ever. Crushing it, Ruby!

Finding besties in your new place is a good indication that you have simultaneously committed to your new environment and asserted your true self in it. For a while, you may think it won't happen. But you'll meet a few people who stick around. You'll have running gags. You'll know their garage code. You will spend minor holidays with the new friends, then mini-vacations, then maybe maxi ones. Over time, you will know when their parents are sick, when their kids are graduating, and when their chickens get eaten by foxes—not because you saw it on Facebook or heard it out your bedroom window—but because they told you, and they were sad, and someone losing their pet chicken to a fox doesn't seem all that funny to you anymore. Over the years, all of those Mayberry moments will add up to a life.

Back in the Adjustment phase section, when we talked about how to stop whining to random red state nurses, I told you things would be different when you found your peeps. I said that your *real* friends would actually want to hear your self-indulgent stories or at least listen without rolling their eyes or wincing. And that's true. Sometimes I feel like my bicultural perspective even helps them! One of my townie friends, for example, is an "iron man," which means he exercises like, three hours a day. I mock him relentlessly for this and make sarcastic jabs at his expense whenever possible. He tolerates this because, well, he has to—our kids are friends. But he's also benefited, at times, from my straight talk.

One autumn, for example, he said he was "drowning" in all his responsibilities—how was he expected to be able to rake his massive piles of leaves, cook meals for his children, drive them to compete in all of their athletic events, and manage his personal life? Based on my experience, I said, he had three options: One, he could hire people. When I was in grad school, I made extra money tutoring rich kids on the Upper East Side of Manhattan. Their families had cooks, nannies, chauffeurs, and personal assistants. It seemed to me that the only tasks those parents had to do themselves were writing checks, shopping at silent auctions, and periodically introducing themselves to their own children. Two, I said, he could do less. This option wasn't realistic for him, either, though, because athletic competitions give him life. This option also sounded hollow coming from me: My helicopter-parenting game was strong, and he knew it. That left him with option three: Stop raking the fucking leaves.

I used to rake leaves, I said, when we first moved back here, and I actually thought yard work might be cool. As the proud owner of a suburban yard, I considered it my duty to keep the place manicured and free of natural debris. I'd rake all weekend long, every weekend, in November. My shoulders ached, my eyes were swollen shut from pollinated dirt. I knew my descent into madness was complete the day I took a broom to the top of my driveway and started *sweeping the street*. Then I came to my senses and found my truth: Raking is for chumps! Yard work, without question, is the scourge of modern suburban life. Just leave it! Or hire, as I now do, an army of men with heavy artillery leaf blowers to blow that shit to the curb. And you know what else I said? Parenting is like raking leaves. No matter how much you rake, you won't get it all done. Some leaves stick to the ground like leaf starch. Some drop late. Some blow down from your tidy little leaf pile and mess up the lawn again. You can sweep them all off your driveway in late fall, but in the spring, under the thawing snow and ice—along with the dead chipmunks and the soggy sticks of sidewalk chalk—you will inevitably find a mushy pile of last autumn's leaves, clumped in between the garage door and that thing that looks like it might be a gas meter. There's no blue ribbon waiting for you at your grave for the best suburban leaf pile. Embrace the imperfection, iron man.

My adjustment has made me wiser, and I like to think it's helped my friends adjust, too. One friend of mine, for example, really hates being around sick people. It bugs her when people show up to Thanksgiving dinner after their kids just got over a bad flu and they're coughing all over the pie. Or at synagogue, when someone sits next to her with their coat on and a pack of Kleenex in one hand. She asked me how she should handle her feelings. What would I say to someone like this?

Since I've spent years in Wisconsin trying to figure out when it's worthwhile to speak my mind—and when I should keep bitchy comments about swine flu to myself—I told her what I honestly thought. One of our biggest challenges as humans is coping with the selfish or annoying people around us. Sometimes, we do have to speak our mind. My kids played soccer for a while after we moved here, for example, until they realized soccer involves running. At one game, this loudmouth dad from the other team was gloating and cheering and keeping score, and while I understood his issue—he was wearing a Yankees cap and hadn't adjusted yet—you aren't supposed to keep score at a kindergarten soccer game. It's like, an actual rule. Someone needed to tell him to shut up. So I did. And eventually, I'm sure he appreciated it.

But other things are out of our control! Back in New York, for example, we had a neighbor, Richard, who ran his business out of his apartment. He rode everywhere on this old *Wizard of Oz* bicycle. We liked him a lot, but he hung up his bike—bike*s*, actually—on the wall of our fire escape. It was our only means of egress other than the front door. We talked to Richard about it. We talked to Alfredo about it. Alfredo spoke to Richard. Richard would move the bikes over. But he didn't take them out altogether, or if he did, he would do so temporarily and they would reappear. Should we have yelled and screamed and ruined our otherwise decent neighborly relationship? Should I have dumped the other neighbor's cigarette butts on his doormat too? Not worth it. Eventually, we threw our hands up and just put our strollers on the fire escape, too.

And that's what I told my bugged friend. It's one thing to yell at a blowhard on a soccer field who can't turn down his competitive impulses, but quite another to yell at someone at your religious congregation, or the neighbor guy—yes, he caused a fire trap, but his employees gave me cream for my coffee when I ran out! I mean, people have idiosyncrasies. Here, we live in a neighborhood where dudes get their panties in a twist if you toss something in their curbside garbage can. Like it's sacred space that might get sullied by your discarded coffee cup. Go yell about germs if you want, I told my friend. Ask them to move to another row, or stay home next Thanksgiving. But in the end, you probably won't change much behavior. Meanwhile, they may never speak to you again. In Wisconsin, they might even pull out their concealed weapon, which is actually worse than catching a cold.

Before we shut down this good neighbor festival, I want to pass along one more insight to help demystify the process of Mastery. According to my mom, and probably other experts, psychologists have long debated which vegetable best describes the human concept of self. If you thought people stopped comparing humans to vegetables after they were born, think again! Some psychologists believe we're like onions, a compilation of our different roles and skills and lifestyles layered on top of each other. I believe—and so does my mom—that we are more like artichokes. We have layers of identity, which reflect the multiplicity of our choices and experience, but deep down, we have a steady heart, a core self that is meaty and solid and extra delicious when dipped in mayonnaise.

Unless we have been beaten down by life circumstances or extremely adverse childhood experiences, our core selves stay strong and intact, no matter where we go. Perhaps your core self was drawn to life in a big city, where you discovered its magnificent wholeness and potential for boundless expression. That city added new layers of culture and meaning and insight to your experience. And leaving that cool city was a big change.

You developed new layers as you adjusted. You discovered that part of you that enjoys quietude, or even the woods. But your heart remained, basically, the same.

From time to time, an old friend in New York asks me how we're adjusting to our new life. Just kidding. They never ask me anything. Frankly, I'm not sure some of our old friends even know where we live. I suspect they think we just moved downtown to enroll our kids in a magnet school, and they can't visit because it would mean changing trains at Times Square.

If they did ask, though, I would tell them that my heart still longs for the city like Marley longs for the ocean and Hanna longs for brown rice. So Mike and I visit New York a lot. We miss it. But we like it here, too. We're artichokes that way.

Chapter 11

TELLING THE PO-PO WHAT THEY NEED TO KNOW

YEARS INTO HER relocation, it's still complicated for "Marley." She likes Madison, especially the lakes. She and her husband bought a boat, and they love being on the water, except when he insists on staying out all day long and then she calls it the "boat dungeon." Still, even now, she often feels a little thrown off her bearings. "Without the tide lapping outside the window to mark the passage of time" and the "lithium raising off the saltwater into air" to steady her out, she doesn't feel quite like herself. Before she shared these feelings, I didn't know about the lithium in the sea salt. And I don't know if she's right about the air. When she's sad now, I just say some platitude like, *if only we had those lithium vapors*, just to sort of validate her feelings.

But true story: Even gurus lose their shit sometimes. Remember how the Adjustment phase has ups and downs? Well, the Mastery phase has been a perpetual work in progress for me, too. We feel pretty embedded here. We follow the golden rule of both mental health *and* good neighboring—boundaries, boundaries, boundaries. But we still talk about going back. And I dread the idea that one of my close friends might leave. "Hanna" and I once had a low-level snit about it, which basically dragged on until she decided to stay. Sometimes I'm just bummed out about aging, and it freaks me out that my new friends live in houses where I used to smoke pot in high school, and I start obsessing that my adventure clock is running down and I've never been to Bora-Bora.

As we move through the nuances of cultural mastery, remember that getting over culture shock is not a sprint, it's a marathon. And sometimes it's a marathon you *wanted* to run but never actually *signed up* for because the website triggered some weird old insecurities about high school track and field, so you waited four years to register and then only did it because someone made you. Of course I'm talking about my driver's license. The whole ordeal unfolded like the stages of grief.

I. DENIAL

Everyone has their own reasons for pretending they don't have to do something. For some people, it's laziness. For others, it's fear. For me, it was both of those things plus—if I'm being perfectly honest—vanity. I liked the hawt picture on my old license.

At some point, many years ago, the New York DMV renewed my license without taking a new photograph. I mean, the lighting wasn't that great and the picture was grainy, but otherwise, I looked *ah-mazing*. That picture was taken a *long time ago*. Like, before I had kids. Before aging, sleep deprivation, and years of sarcastic facial expressions had eroded my wrinkles into face trenches. Give up a picture of myself taken when I was thirty and living the dream in New York? In exchange for a picture of me at x-number of years older than that, when I've become a suburban Klingon in a fleece?

Why that picture hibernated for so long in the DMV database is one of the world's great unsolved mysteries. It's up there with why Chuck E. Cheese's always smells like beer farts, why people believe in the "good old days" when they obviously sucked, and why husbands can never find things they are "looking" for. But whatever the mystical reason was, I wasn't about to give my license up just because I'd settled in another part of the country and written law required it.

It was easy to live in this state of denial, too, because I didn't actually use the license that often. Quick 411 to the kids out there—nobody cards you in your late thirties except Whole Foods. They have one of those liquor policies where the clerks have to card anyone who isn't their actual own grandma. "Oh, sure," I said the first time, pulling out my New York license. "Are you also carding old pregnant bitches in here now?" I was quoting Craig Robinson's joke from *Knocked Up*. I guess the clerk didn't get it.

Of course, I *liked* showing my old New York license to the Whole Foods clerk. It reinforced my denial and massaged my ego. If you think I am the only fragile middle-aged lady to wrestle with vanity like this, I'll pass on what Marley told me. It took her four years to get a new license, too. Why? "Because my hair looked great in my Maine license. It was good for eight years! I was so young in that picture!" She cried when she finally switched over, and said the new picture is "more or less a mug shot in which I look like a dried-up old farm-town hooker." If that quotation doesn't explain our bond of friendship, nothing ever will.

2. ANGER

Once I got past the fear and the vanity—or rather, started to fear that my vanity was becoming too transparent—I got angry. I get too angry pretty easily; just ask Mike. Yes, I may have moved here, *by choice*. I have friends here now, and call it *home*. But the New York license, like New York itself, is way more awesome than the Wisconsin one. Mine was shimmery and pink. Pink, motherfuckers! It had aqua lettering, for no apparent reason, except maybe to celebrate gay pride. Or the ocean. Or both. Either way, I was *into* it. It was queer and here and near the pretend lithium vapor, just like New York.

My Wisconsin license is the opposite of that in every possible way. It looks like a membership card for the Nature Conservancy. It has tiny images of a sailboat, a sunset, a red barn, and some green foliage that looks like it was pulled from a children's book. But not in a good way. More like if Kevin Henkes, Caldecott-winning children's book author and illustrator, was drunk-scribbling on a cocktail napkin while watching a Packers game. The images are so sincere and earnest that every time I look at the license, I just want to buy a log cabin on a northern lake and hang myself from the rafters with a fishing line. Just kidding. I wouldn't even know where to buy fishing line.

There are birds on it, too. Not a dirty pigeon pecking at the crusts of an old sandwich on top of a trash can, or the local equivalent of that, which is a mean old goose or a badass hawk. The birds don't even look like the big fat fucking turkeys that actually walk around our neighborhood in gangs of seven, scratching the shit out of everyone's mulch. These birds, the Wisconsin license birds, are just maudlin and cartoonish, like they are soaring high in the sky on their way to their final destination, which is a cheesy pamphlet for a drug recovery center. So basically, if you need an identification card to get you into a sustainability conference or a twelve-step program, Wisconsin is your place.

The American flag is fine. I've always considered myself a patriot. Not the ass-out flag-waving kind, just the kind that doesn't collude with foreign adversaries and repress the vote to win elections. But I'm good with a flag on an ID card. This set me apart from Hanna, who didn't like any of it. She had changed her license right away, though. "Ripped off the Band-Aid," as she put it, "but it hurt. They made me surrender my California license and gave me a stupid one with a little red barn in the corner." Again, there you have it.

3. BARGAINING

If you're sassy and vain, and it takes you a couple years to get past the fact that you look old as fuck and Alcoholics Anonymous designed the state license, there is only one way to go. Start bargaining for time. In my case, the bargaining was about trying to avoid—for as long as possible—the DMV.

In big urban areas and definitely New York, going to the DMV is like traveling to an authoritarian third world country. Our DMV office in New York was down in Herald Square, right near the Macy's department store. On busy weekend days, that Macy's is a bit like a third world country, too, one that's massively overpopulated by people who never hang up their clothes. The only safe house in that whole midtown terrain was the Mrs. Fields Cookies, which—let's face it—is the New York dessert equivalent of the lunch counter at Target.

I've always wondered why more filmmakers didn't shoot spy thrillers in that DMV. You wouldn't even need a set designer. Check it out: Trained mercenaries are dispatched to rescue an agent who's being held in a grungy midtown basement. Using their reconnaissance skills, they follow the obscure signs to the back of the cavernous building, pack themselves into a small dilapidated elevator, then emerge into a vast, foul-smelling, drab room. Believe me when I say this, Reader: If you took out the benches in there and tied Daniel Craig to a chair—ideally shirtless, with droplets of water falling from the ceiling—you would absolutely believe he'd been captured by SPECTRE.

The last time I was renditioned to the Herald Square DMV, I was there to register my car. It was a hot summer day, and I was about nine and a half months pregnant. The fact that I still owned a car was already stupid. Like most people who lived in Manhattan, we almost never used it. But since we already owned it and were perpetually trying to figure out how to leave, we paid a parking garage six hundred dollars a month just so we didn't have to deal with the fuckery of alternate-side parking. Once a month or so, I ran into one of the comics from *The Daily Show*—name omitted to protect the innocent—who parked his car at the same facility. It was still bonkers.

After waiting approximately three thousand minutes in the airless basement of that DMV, it was my turn at the window. I waddled up to the appropriate blinking number and told the agent I wanted to register my car. She took my papers, looked them over, and told me that I couldn't register the car in New York until I paid the New York sales tax. Why didn't I know this before walking up there with my overstuffed abdomen? Because I had bought that fucking car in another state!

"But I didn't buy it here," I said, wishing I could break my water all over her number eight cubby. I pointed to the bill of sale, which clearly indicated I had purchased it in Cranston, Rhode Island. Just looking at that receipt gave me PTSD about the c-word lady. Unfortunately for me, it turns out you can't legally leave the state of New York—for anything less than a year—and come back with a car. As far as New York is concerned, the *only reason* you said good-bye to your friends, rented an apartment in another state, earned a salary there, paid taxes to that state, and filed an insurance claim when someone rear-ended you, called you the c-word, and then gave you false papers was to screw New York out of their nine percent sales tax.

"The only reason I came back again," I explained, "was because I got pregnant!" Telling a perfect stranger at the DMV that you got knocked up is not considered TMI in New York. It's just a business transaction. I offered to get a letter from my former employer or landlord.

That wouldn't help, she told me. "Those are the rules. You should've gotten a Rhode Island driver's license."

Cue the dripping water.

4. DEPRESSION

After getting past the vanity, the red barn, and DMV-driven delays, I got sort of woeful about it. Identity cards are just tiny tokens of place. They're the human version of cat tags. For people who experience discrimination at the hands of the right-wing

state, they are now called "voter ID cards." Whatever you call
them, they're just the regulatory process by which the state
certifies our legal privileges, traces our criminal behavior, and
keeps track of which organs the ER doctors can yank out after
a fatal car accident.

This would have been a really good time for me to remember
that getting over culture shock is a marathon, not a sprint. But
when you're feeling insecure about your identity, little changes
take on exaggerated meaning. My license felt like a tiny reflec-
tion of my inner self, the last remaining marker of who I had
been at an earlier, younger, more promising time in my life. It
proved my New York identity to store clerks so I didn't have to
justify why I was swearing. And when I looked at that pretty
pink license in my wallet, I still felt connected to my coura-
geous and carefree past. I'm being slightly melodramatic about
this, Reader, but I'd been carrying around a New York license
with that picture for most of my adult life. It lived in my pocket-
book longer than all of those rubbish one-cent postage stamps
that I couldn't bring myself to toss, and the ATM receipts that
kept getting stuck in the zipper of my change purse. Getting old
can be depressing, and no offense to Wisconsin, but Wisconsin
was making it worse.

People get weird about giving up their cell phone numbers
for the same reason. I was talking about the *Seinfeld* sweatpants
episode earlier; remember the one about area codes? In that
episode, a man in the park asks Elaine if her 646 number is from
New Jersey. Drama ensues. A similar debacle happened with
the new 347 area code in the first *Sex and the City* movie, too.
There's a reason New Yorkers keep writing sitcoms about area
codes. Because they're running out of material. Or because

status and identity are important things to New Yorkers. Or because human beings don't like stuff to change, because it reminds us that we're all going to die.

5. ACCEPTANCE

What finally forced me to do the right thing? The same thing that kills all juvenile fantasies: marriage. Basically, I felt like a bad wife. And I don't say that very often. I cook awesome food. I wash my hair pretty regularly. I didn't change my name when I got married, but on the other hand, I didn't change my mind about being married, either, not even when Mike copped to guzzling all that milk.

Being a lawyer and such an upstanding guy in general, Mike surrendered his out-of-state license immediately. He cited "the law." Personally, I think laws are interpretive. I approached the license law more like a "helpful suggestion," which is also how I view the spot for hybrid cars in the Whole Foods parking lot. I park my regular car there all the time. Not only because those spaces are arbitrary entitlements, but because my refusal to play along really rankles the hippies. Mike thinks I'm a dick when I park there, especially since that time I drove his car and his battery died and he had to sit there—in his flagrantly non-hybrid car, in the hybrid spot—waiting for the guy with jumper cables.

If anyone should've been clinging to the trappings of our former life, it was Mike. The whole Wisconsin thing was totally my idea. He *hates* winter. During our first winter here, the weather through much of January was in the double negative digits. Mike was using a lot of double negatives of his own that

year. He'd say things like: "There isn't a day I don't regret
moving here" or "I can't imagine a less appealing place to live."
Then we saw a story in the newspaper about an old Norwegian
woman in Minnesota who slipped on some ice. She got stuck
in a frozen snowbank for several hours and temporarily lost
her heartbeat. After several hours in the hospital, she was
revived and woke as robust as ever. Mike was equally intrigued
and horrified by her cryogenic miracle.

"See," I told him, trying to put a positive spin on it. "It's so
cold in the Midwest, you can't even *die*."

He wasn't adjusting as easily as I was, in some ways, but he
had mastered the ability to follow the law. Ultimately, three
things pushed me over the edge. First of all, my license had
the wrong address on it. If I got into an accident, someone
would need to contact Mike and tell him where all the pots
and pans go. Also, we had bought that Subaru. If he lost his
job—or he ultimately decided he couldn't handle the winter—
I was *not* going to pay that motherfucking New York sales tax
again.

Second, my identity card was starting to make me feel like I
was lying. In New York, gaming the system is part of survival.
Everyone does it. Living a lie in the suburbs feels worse, though,
because there's no anonymity. When someone here is having an
affair, everyone hears about it. About five minutes before it happens.
That's because when someone is cheating, there's a good chance
that the cheater *and* his mistress *and* his spouse belong to the
same community pool or do hot yoga together on weekends.
Good luck sneaking off to a local hotel for an illicit rendez-
vous, dawg, your wife is already there for the scrapbooking
convention.

When I finally switched, it was because my license was about to expire. Readers, living a lie was bad. But having to take that written test again would have been a fucking *catastrophe*. I don't follow a lot of the driving rules, even if I *do* remember them. So one day in the spring, I dug some lipstick out of the garbage at the bottom of my fleece pocket and marched down to the DMV, the same office where I'd gotten my very first driver's license at the age of sixteen. Hashtag: #Truetownietales.

It was no Herald Square rendition site. Some of the same people might have worked there, but it had been updated several times. It was practically empty. It was also clean, organized, and open to natural light, and everyone who worked there—with the possible exception of the photographer, whose response to my *one* question about where to stand was that I was "making this harder than it had to be"—seemed to be on the right side of humanity's survival.

That's not to say it all worked out. I had been living a double life that I didn't even *know* about! The manager told me they had two separate records for me in the system—one for my current residence and one associated with my childhood home.

"I'm sorry," she said, sounding truly sorry. "You'll have to come back in a few days, after our IT department can unify them."

I left feeling relieved. I didn't want my bloody corpse to be mistaken for someone else—or my live body to be turned away from voting—because of an IT error. Even more important, when I got back to the car I realized that in my haste to prepare for the picture, I had smeared lipstick all over my teeth. Maybe that's what the cranky photographer meant.

A few weeks later, we went up to the Dells for my nephew's sixth birthday party. My sister said he had always wanted to have a party at a water park. I'm pretty sure she chose it just to get back at me for pushing her down the stairs when she was a baby. Either way, she got her revenge, because on the way home, a sheriff guy pulled me over for speeding.

It was a routine white person traffic stop, but it quickly escalated into a clusterfuck. First, I couldn't find our insurance papers. I handed the guy some expired ones and apologized. He said that in addition to the speeding ticket, he'd have to fine me for having expired insurance papers. Then he asked me for my driver's license. I gave him my New York license, which I still hadn't relinquished. The conversation went something like this:

"So, you're visiting from out of town?"

"No. But we just moved back here."

"Uh-huh. When did you move back?"

"Um. About three years ago. Almost four. I know—I mean—I tried—I went there to get the new one. But my identity wasn't, like, unified in their system. She said to come back. I just haven't gotten back there yet." The sheriff guy went back to sit in his car for a while, which is always the scariest part, because I am really bad at waiting. I'm bad at sweating, too. I don't know why. I think it's an Irish thing.

I didn't mention to the sheriff that the license snafu had only happened two weeks ago. I didn't mention it because he didn't ask. As far as I'm concerned, if the police need to know something, they will ask. Otherwise, you have the right to remain silent, which I interpret to mean that unless they ask, the po-po don't need to know. In the Catholic church, this would be considered a lie. But truth be told, lying doesn't bother me nearly as much as patriarchy does, and the church lets that slide every Sunday.

By the time he got back to the window, the universe had worked it all out for me. Basically, my kids started to fight in the backseat. Like really fight, in that screaming, name-calling, I-hate-you kind of way which—if you weren't sitting in a car, stopped by a sheriff—would make you open a bottle of wine and pour the whole thing down your piehole. I don't know if he felt sorry for me, lost his train of thought, or just wanted to get the hell away from my asshole children, but he only fined me ten dollars for expired insurance. He gave me a stern warning on the speeding and told me to go back—first thing next week— to "get that license changed." I didn't mention that while he was sitting back in his vehicle, I had found the updated insurance papers. I didn't want him to change his mind about the ticket.

The following week—to keep the universe in balance, and myself out of jail—I went back to the DMV. I got the Wisconsin license. It has—and I'm truly not exaggerating—the worst picture of me that I have ever seen. It doesn't even look like me. It actually looks like a woman I used to share an apartment with in Brooklyn, whose name was Meghan and—now that I see it on the card—looked like a pale, more startled version of my future self. I accepted my karmic payback and walked out.

WHAT DOES MY tale of woe teach us about Mastery? If you're a practical, law-abiding type of attorney-person like my husband—or have real reasons to fear legal persecution—then, nothing. The license debacle taught me something about myself, though. It really did. It reaffirmed for me that change is part of life. We all change, sometimes in subtle, trivial, token ways and sometimes in more meaningful and substantial ones. We promote or conceal parts of ourselves, sometimes from minute to minute, depending on where we are and who we're with.

Yet no matter how much our lives change on the outside—or how ugly and depressing your new license is—we all have that authentic self, our artichoke heart, that doesn't actually change that much. I decided to stop cursing at the grocery store because I didn't want to make old ladies uncomfortable. Particularly my own mom. But I'm always going to be an irreverent, sarcastic person who discloses my feelings and bucks the system a little bit. I just am. That's why I love New York. That's probably why I stayed there so long, with my sweet, sweet 646 area code.

In a way, going native is like the serenity prayer: Change what you can, accept what you can't, and be wise enough to know when it's time to stop lying to the cops. Go get it, Reader, and live your best life. No seriously, go get it. You might need it to vote.

Chapter 12

LIVING (PARTS OF) THE
SUBURBAN DREAM

ANOTHER FUN TWIST in the gauntlet of cultural mastery
is that people are different. Going native means different
things for different people, even in the same place. You may love
the cost of living and the vibrant black community in Atlanta
but really not love the crazy thunderstorms and the traffic. On
the other hand, some people love thunderstorms, and I know this
because they post storm cloud pictures on Instagram all day and
night. Here's another info-nugget I picked up: drunk *biking* isn't
illegal. I've seen that on Instagram, too. As you can see, I live a
very full life.

Some people argue that embracing winter sports is a necessary precondition to finding serenity in cold climates. Wisconsin
denizens are particularly obsessed with finding ways to spend
the long cold winters, and I think their instinct is basically
right. Some of the available options for winter recreation will
never appeal to me, because hockey rinks are chilly, chairlifts
go too high off the ground, and we can't travel every weekend
because Mike won't let me buy airplane seats for our cats. But
figuring out which regional activities work for you—and which
you cannot abide—is an important step in going native.

WATER PARKS!

Who doesn't love splashing around indoors in the winter, in warm, heavily chlorinated water? The kiddies love water parks. The Wisconsin Dells, the world's largest water park town, is the perfect place to visit for birthdays, gymnastics team retreats, and couples from Illinois who want their kids kept busy while they get sloshed on rail tequila and fruit-tinted corn syrup. The Dells has something for everyone! Long hallways. Wild unsupervised teens, running. Tats on tats. Air hockey. Ropes courses. Saggy men with no pants. Anything in the world you might want, except clams.

I'm glad that people who go there to lift their winter malaise find it helpful. Personally, however, I find it physically painful to walk into a safari-themed hotel that has restless hordes of nine-year-old boys playing laser tag, white girls getting cornrows, and caged baby tigers in the lobby, available for rental-petting. The last time I drove up there, I went so deep into the water park pain, I started praying for a zombie attack so I wouldn't have to drown myself in the lazy river. Then, I realized, that was not an unrealistic fantasy.

According to apocalypse experts, humankind will be overrun by its basest elements and vanquished by the undead. The basest elements include a loose grouping of men who follow the Paleo Diet, Patriots fans, and people who still use the phrase "Indian giver." First, they'll overtake the water parks. If zombies know what's good for them—and I think they do—they will attack highly populated areas to get their early recruits. Any single water park in the Dells, in the off-season, probably holds ten thousand people, not counting the people who snuck in without a paper bracelet. From the moment you leave your hotel room, at exactly nine o'clock in the morning, you are swept up in a human tidal wave of shoeless adults and wailing children in swim diapers that is so vast, you instinctively begin scanning the hallway for search-and-rescue teams from the Red Cross. To wit: They are never there.

Inside the water park compound—which looks suspiciously similar to Home Depot—the zombies will wait until just the right time to mount a sneak attack. Technically speaking, they won't even have to sneak. Between the air guns, the rushing water, the industrial ceiling fans, and all the people screaming over all of these other noises, you can't hear a fucking thing. After two hours in there with my sister, Caroline, our voices were hoarse from yelling basic conversational phrases at each other's faces. I'd say to my sister: "I'M GOING TO THE BATHROOM!" Then she'd say, "WHAT?!" Then I'd say, "YOU TAKE THE KIDS DOWN THE SLIDE AGAIN!" Then she'd say, "WHAT?!!" We cherished this time together and will never forget about the time we got together to yell, until one of us gave up and staggered out to the giant communal hot tub. Or as our mom calls it, the large outdoor toilet.

Once the zombies start bearing down on people, chaos will reign. Other than the lifeguards—who are teenagers and are hired to save people from the lazy river and not zombies nobody who works at the Dells cares about you. In that sense, it's *exactly* like Home Depot. Last time, when I checked in, I asked the woman handing me two hundred water park maps if the rooms had flatware for dining. She said, "I couldn't tell you that." She *couldn't?* Because she didn't know? Or because she didn't give a flying fuck if I lived or died one more day, with or without flatware? Good talk, team. Let's catch up after the zombie emergency.

Ultimately, the zombies will win because you will voluntarily surrender to them at the end of your long day at the water park. After several water slides, a go-kart ride, a game of laser tag with the mercenary nine-year-olds, and some good old-fashioned Skee-Ball, our kids asked if we could do the ropes course. After the ropes course—which, as an aside, is actually pretty good training for the zombie apocalypse—we were so exhausted that we didn't even want to go out to dinner. We just crawled back to the room to order pizza (PS: no flatware). My sister was sick with a cold and collapsed. I drank heavily, because if the undead are gonna take me, they are not taking me sober.

BASEMENTS!

Four years in, we decided to remodel our basement. Admittedly, that surprised a few people who had heard me say, on numerous occasions, that I *would never remodel that fucking basement*. I probably said that back in the Honeymoon phase, when I was still juiced about the laundry room and thought Robert Downey Jr. was at the public library. Back then, I still thought I'd *walk* to the grocery store. What? People only walk here if they are wearing athletic clothing! If you walk down a suburban street in regular clothes, you risk being mistaken for a streetwalker, or someone who just ran out of gas. And heaven forbid you run into someone and kiss them on the cheek—as you might in New York—to say hello. You might as well just wear a sandwich board that says I BELONG TO A GAY PARISIAN ARTIST CULT.

Our neighbors, meanwhile, seemed to spend an inordinate amount of time in their basements. Like, I'd go down there sometimes to get the American flag or drain the dehumidifier, but our basement wasn't a place you'd want to linger. It flooded a lot, the insulation was falling out of the walls, the floors were made of asbestos, it smelled like a rodent morgue, and after really hard rainstorms, the rusted Kohler laundry sink looked like a tiny skate park for centipedes. It was also, I'd hasten to add, underground. *Under* the ground. New Yorkers don't hang out underground unless they lucked into a cheap "garden-level" apartment, are doing the laundry, are drinking sake at a Japanese speakeasy, or are mole people.

The mole people are an impoverished subculture of people who live 100 percent underground. In New York, they allegedly live in the subway tunnels. Someone wrote a book about their primitive, subterranean society, which was well received, until other experts who study primitive subterranean societies said the book was based on a whole bunch of evidence which—like the mole people themselves—never actually surfaced. So, I guess, make your own informed decisions about that. What I learned from reading about the controversy was that mole people actually exist all over the country. Homeless drug addicts in Las Vegas, for example, live in the sewer system to escape the searing temperatures. I find that truly sad, but given that thousands of people sit inside casinos all day to escape the heat while feeding multiple forms of addiction, it's not necessarily even the saddest thing about Las Vegas.

But the Wisconsin mole people have their own, very solid reasons for spending the winter underground. Before you leave a city and purchase a suburban home, you can't possibly fathom how much shit 1) needs to be fixed and 2) is in the basement. Think of it this way: Your new house is the size of an actual apartment building, but it doesn't come stocked with a staff of dedicated people to go into the basement to fix things. You can hire people to service shit in your basement in Wisconsin, but they probably won't agree to live in your house. Not until you take down that yard sign, anyway.

Consider the story of our furnace. One year on Thanksgiving, we all went to my sister's house. Unfortunately, I didn't get to catch up with that nurse, but it was still a great time. My brother-in-law brined and grilled a twenty-three-pound turkey, despite having had knee surgery the day before. My sister said he had torn his knee fishing, which sounded either apocryphal or really clumsy. "You just can't sneak up on trout," he explained, "unless you're really crouching." We nodded. And we would've loved to hear more, but our furnace died and we had to rush back home. Reader, I'm not telling you this because it's an exciting story. But as "Hanna" once observed, you can't live in Wisconsin without spending a significant portion of every winter talking about furnaces and fireplaces. It's like gutters and deer carcasses. That's just where the action is.

Over time, I stopped judging the ways of the Wisconsin mole people and accepted that they're doing what mole people do. They take refuge underground to escape extreme weather. They often suffer from temporary or chronic mental illness, exacerbated by an extreme deficiency of vitamin D. My mom once told me that you could spend all day outside in the winter, completely naked, and still not get enough vitamin D from the sun. Not sure how she knows stuff like that. But if that's true, I thought, why not just stay in the basement, with clothes on? That's why people hibernate from November to late May; then the arctic vortex finally recedes and everyone immediately turns on their air-conditioning.

In an atavistic nod to the primitive nature of these underground spaces, some people call them "man caves." To me, that seems sexist. But women have had it too good for too long. I suppose I should just be glad I'm not a homestead wife who has to put on a corset and slaughter a pig. That whale bone was *tight*, bitches. Don't start.

Maybe it's a good thing that basements give local residents a safe place in which to pickle themselves for the long winter ahead. We once passed a guy on the highway who'd been pulled over for a sobriety test. I don't know if he had his insurance card—or even a driver's license—but he was failing the sobriety test miserably. It was nine A.M. In many states—with the possible exception of some parts of Massachusetts and Hartford, Connecticut—when men get drunk and become verbally abusive toward others on social media, it's called alcoholism. In Wisconsin, it's called a hockey game. Do us all a favor, tough guys: Stay in the man caves. Forever.

My first few winters here, I insisted on living *above* the ground, like a fully evolved human being. I read books by firelight. I mulled wine. We kept our nearly nonexistent porch lights on, hoping a neighbor might stop by after a spontaneous snowshoe adventure. What happened was, I just spent those long four-hour days looking out the window, alone. The only actual people I saw had round bodies and noses made of stumpy carrots. Or maybe those were snowmen. Hard to tell after three P.M., when the sun had already gone down.

When I did finally renovate the basement, it wasn't for the furnace technician or the mental illness or the winter pickling. It was about extreme springtime weather, and it was my parents' fault.

THE BASEMENT OF my childhood home was basically a root cellar, which is a pioneer term for a concrete hole in the ground. My parents used that basement—and still do—for three main purposes:

1. *Laundry, auxiliary fridge, and storage.* Sometimes my mom would ask me to run down to the basement to get something—like a pint of ice cream or a laundry basket or a poisonous biting spider—and I'd run down as fast as I could, praying that a monster wouldn't eat my face off before I yanked the requested item out of the cobwebs. That sounds juvenile, but in my defense, I was literally a juvenile. Also, my dad was an early adopter of energy-saving lightbulbs, so it was like the dark-sky ordinance down there. Luckily, there was a crawl space at the bottom of the stairs that my parents literally referred to as the "monster closet." Because the term "crawl space" wasn't creepy enough.

2. *Breeding a rodent super-race.* Remember that book *Mrs. Frisby and the Rats of NIMH* about the lab rats who went rogue and saved field mice? My dad read that to us and I loved it. Coincidentally, one winter my older brother got some white lab mice. They were so intelligent, they

figured out how to escape from their cage. Everyone presumed them dead until the following spring, when my dad spotted a number of mice in the basement that were half-brown and half-white. We all wondered: *Were they a super-race of country and city mice, extra bookish and street-smart, like the NIMH rats?* Then they all ate the poison and died. So I guess we got our answer.

3. *Tornadoes.* During severe weather events, of which there are many here in the farthest northern reaches of Tornado Alley, everyone in Wisconsin piles into their root cellars. Well, almost everyone. When I was growing up, whenever the siren sounded, my dad would shepherd all the kids down into the basement to huddle together in front of the monster closet. My mom—I guess because she grew up in the city and never saw *The Wizard of Oz*—refused to join us. She'd sit upstairs next to the large picture window in the living room, reading a book. Yeah, the house might have been swept away, but *whatever,* she had a mystery book to read and those energy-saving lightbulbs just didn't cut it. Looking back, her stubbornness taught me that book club is the better part of valor. But it also taught us that the only thing worse than being dragged down into a crawl space full of cobwebs and dead supermice is worrying that your mother will be killed by a tornado before finishing *The No. 1 Ladies' Detective Agency.*

As a result of this marital game of chicken, my sister and I are both heinously afraid of tornadoes. At the slightest rumble of thunder, both of us hurl a flashlight, two packs of batteries, a weather radio, some fleeces, several bags of dried fruit, an anxiety blanket, and all of our children down the basement stairs. We never realized we both suffered from tornadophobia until we both moved back here—over the same summer—and bought our first suburban homes. Hers was near a cornfield, which was extra terrifying. But that phobia truly is, more than anything, what led me to renovate the basement. Because if a supercell is about to level our house—or fell a fifty-ton oak tree onto the roof—I'd rather be sitting comfortably on an Ikea couch, drinking Korbel and eating Scott's spreadable cheese, than hiding under an anxiety blanket in a monster closet. Who knows best? The Wisconsin mole people do.

Chapter 13

LOSING YOUR KIDS IN
THE WOODS

Way back in the Judgment phase, I delineated some of the most common areas of culture shock, which included things like communication, food, dress codes, and political views. We haven't drilled down into parenting, and there's a reason for that. Apart from politics, it's the scariest category! And unlike driving, parenting doesn't require a license. For most of us, parenting is the easiest to judge and hardest to master.

Mike and I have pretty much mastered the school situation here. As I've mentioned, we are so grateful to be able to send our children to the quality public schools. We don't have to drive luxury cars into rivers, and both kids can attend school in the same district. Still, as we muddled our way through every policy—from individualized learning to the outlawing of Halloween—we realized that there is just no perfect school, even in suburbs with stable tax bases and livable teacher salaries. All parents have to figure out how and when to intervene in their kids' problems at school. But coming from a more competitive educational culture, it took me a long time to find the right balance between taking initiative and acting like a complete *noodge.* Now that I've mastered it, I'm a superpolite noodge. But other aspects of parenting have been more challenging. Disagreements about parenting aren't just awkward, they're deeply personal. Do you and your best friend ever talk about that time you got crazy mad because her teenage daughter wore a low-cut cocktail dress to your daughter's first communion? Of course you don't, because she's not your best friend anymore.

Parenting styles differ across the country, and I've been struggling to acclimate myself to all the local trends. I really don't want to let my kids roam free, poking deer carcasses in the woods by day and stumbling around on the pitch-black streets by night. As my iron man friend knows, my helicopter game is strong. And I like it that way. I really prefer to supervise my kids' activities and structure their time.

Helicopter parenting is a ubiquitous issue on parenting sites and online journals. Experts often say that giving kids too much supervision is a creepy social disease practiced by control freaks. Back when we were young, they say, we just played outside. We weren't on such rigid schedules. We made our own fun. I gathered from these articles that *making* your own fun is better than just *having* it. In many ways, this reminds me of spending time with my Polish grandmother in Chicago. We always had to make our own fun there, too, because Grandma Stephanie was usually busy going to church, cooking holiday meat, and saving rubber bands for the next world war. Except the people who write these articles probably don't tie plastic scarves over their heads like my grandma did, or tell people to stop jogging because their calves look bulky. I know what my grandma meant was *enough. Bulky enough.*

Both urban and suburban people worry about the effects of helicopter parenting. One of my neighbors alluded to the problem the other day, when we stopped to talk to each other on the street. "I think it has become a real issue for college kids," she said, gesturing at an imaginary college kid with a bag of dog poop. "They don't know how to manage their own downtime." I don't know what her college experience was like. In today's goal-oriented culture, aren't smoking pot, having sex, and taking naps still considered acceptable ways for college kids to manage their downtime? Asking for a friend.

However, it seems like the urbane professional types—whose kids go to Brearley, or proto-segregated charter schools, and are engaged in thousands of supervised extracurricular activities—generate the highest-pitched outcry against helicopter parenting. I'm not bitter about failing to be one of those Brearley parents. Not *that* bitter. But I am skeptical that some of these fancy folks actually know—or remember—what living in a regular place is like.

To get some more background on the problem, I consulted with some of the Internet experts. Apparently, ecopsychologists have railed against helicopter parenting for years. Without unstructured playtime, kids have no way to express their creativity and imagination. As one website put it: Every child is born "sensually whole and bonded to the Earth." Children today need to "recover an integrated sense of themselves in an indoor verbal playground" which "doesn't match one's own internal authentic knowingness." I think I agree with that. But I do have some follow-up questions. What if the term *ecopsychologist* doesn't match *my* internal authentic knowingness? Also, does an indoor verbal playground have to be installed, or does it come fully assembled from Target?

In his book *Manhood for Amateurs*, Pulitzer Prize–winning author Michael Chabon argued that parents today are compensating for the deserted moonscape outside by scheduling more activities for their kids, and that there's no real substitute for the kind of freedom we ourselves enjoyed as children. Reader, I once had the pleasure of producing a local radio interview with Michael Chabon, who I greatly admire—and I really wish I'd come up with the phrase *deserted moonscape*, because it's very creative—but to play devil's advocate, parents didn't used to think there was a real substitute for Tang, either. It turned out—much to the surprise of my entire generation—that kids could just drink real orange juice.

Right before we left New York, a friend gave me a book by Richard Louv, *Last Child in the Woods: Saving Our Children from Nature-Deficit Disorder*. Louv argues that kids today have health problems like obesity and attention disorders because they watch too much TV and do too many organized sports. I read the book in Wisconsin, when the helicopter parenting debate reared up again. There were two reasons for the delay: One is that when people use a phrase like *saving children*—and they do not work for UNICEF, the intensive-care unit, or the coast guard—I suspect they might be fanatics. This is especially true if they are saving children from fake-sounding problems like *nature-deficit disorder*. The other reason was that, because of my bad eyes or the weird font, I thought the book was actually called *Lost* Child in the Woods. I was already afraid of losing my kids every time we went to the park, or the bookstore—I didn't want to find out how dangerous the forest really is.

Louv thinks suburban parents need to stop supervising their kids. He points out that the media—in cahoots with fanatics who talk constantly about saving children—have made us believe that the world is unsafe. Tracking our children's every move may actually *endanger* them, much like—I suppose—turning on the streetlights. In the olden days, Louv says, there used to be more adults around to watch over children. Modern lifestyles have moved a lot of people indoors. It takes a village to raise kids, but these days—if my neighborhood is any indication—the village is busy writing up a co-parenting schedule, or attending key parties, or tracking down the ever-elusive Bookmobile.

Obviously, there are two separate issues in this parenting debate: enjoying more time in nature and engaging in unstructured play. They are closely related, because the nature people would prefer that kids enjoy the nature in unstructured ways. As a suburban dweller, "Abby" understands the nature side. She told me that one of the real downsides of living in a newer development is the absence of nature. They do a lot of skiing, and they love it. "There are amazing mountains and hiking, too," she pointed out. "But they're half-an-hour drive away. At our old house, you could walk out the door and go for a hike." Enjoying nature now feels like something she has to plan ahead of time. And it's always a supervised activity. Like going to Target, but with a gondola instead of an escalator.

We have a lot of nature in our village, right in the backyard. Still, I didn't have the same upbringing as Richard Louv, who seems to have been raised by the Swiss Family Robinson. One of his pet peeves, for example, is that kids today don't *build their own tree houses.* I grew up in this town, and no one in my family had the slightest idea how to build a birdhouse, let alone a tree house. Louv also quotes an elementary school kid who said his parents "don't feel real safe if I'm going too deep in the woods." Really? Not too deep? Not even with a quiver and a compass? Wait—the book actually *is* about losing your children in the woods?

When experts advocate that kids should do fewer structured activities and supervised lessons, I can't escape my urban identity *or* my townie childhood. I grew up on the rural outskirts of what was, back then, a legit small town. I have some very fond memories of being outside in nature. Our house was on a lake. One time, my parents rescued an injured crow from the arboretum and nursed it back to health. Sometimes I'd walk down the block to our neighbor's apple orchard. This guy, Mr. Ashman, often gave kids apples while he tended to his bees. Other days, I'd play by myself in this weird pagoda garden down the street, behind Mrs. Cooper's garage. I don't think she built the pagoda herself, but she was a harp instructor who gave out *full-size candy bars* at Halloween, in the *eighties*. If you'd told me she was the Jade Emperor, I'd have believed it.

When our parents weren't sending us to Mr. Ashman's day care, however, our recreational choices were fairly limited. We rode bikes up and down the street. We rode them to the public beach, where there was sometimes a lifeguard, and always a drug dealer. We laid on towels, then we rode back home. We hit tennis balls against the garage. One day, I sat on the curb for eight straight hours because Van Halen was in town for a show, and the teenage sister of a friend of mine said that David Lee Roth might jog by. We also played a lot of H–O–R–S–E on our sloped driveway. Sometimes we went down to play H–O–R–S–E on our neighbor's flat driveway. As a result of this cognitive enrichment out in nature, I have always been able to spell the word *horse* perfectly.

When developers began turning our quasi-rural block into an actual suburban street, we spent a lot of time playing in the mud piles left over by the construction. One day, my older brother found a big stack of porno magazines. I thought one of the digger trucks had just unearthed them. My brother told me the construction workers had probably just left them there. I don't know how he figured that out. He did play a lot of Dungeons & Dragons. Or maybe it was all those games of H-O-R-S-E.

My friend Michelle knows where I'm coming from, because she grew up in suburban California, not far from where Mike spent his childhood. She sat alone on her swing set a lot, spitting out watermelon seeds. She would hang out in the backyard, swinging and spitting, swinging and spitting. She spent so much time doing this that she now lives with her own children in New York City.

Point is, with all due respect to the nature lovers and helicopter haters, I don't know how much of our unsupervised recreation was all that creative or enriching or restorative. It was fine. We got fresh air. For kids who had crazy parents, it was probably better that they weren't closely supervised. One of my neighborhood friends had a dad who sat around all day on his La-Z-Boy recliner scratching himself with toenails so long they looked like yellow curly fries. He drove a van with dark porthole windows, which he lost years later when the Feds realized he had never paid his taxes. But a lot of the time, having all that freedom to make our own fun was just fucking boring. Parenting experts often say that boredom is no excuse. Being bored can be constructive, and it forces kids to develop creativity. Given how much time I spent being bored as a kid, I expect my Pulitzer Prize will come in the mail any day now.

There were some upsides to playing outdoors all day. You definitely learned to take care of yourself. My sister once crashed into the neighbor's mailbox while riding her bike and fell to the ground unconscious. She thinks it was for several minutes. She doesn't really know how long it was, and I sure don't—I was probably inside the house, bidding on a new bedroom set on *The Price Is Right*! Her friend Katie once got on the city bus by herself and took it all the way out to the mall. She bought a puppy, took it back home on the bus, and hid it in the closet. She was eight years old. I'm sure Katie will always cherish the memory of being able to manage her own free time alone on that restorative city bus ride.

My friends and I spent a lot of time running back and forth across the highway to get to the discount mall behind the McDonald's. We would walk right up the street next to the Antlers Tavern—which was packed with alcoholics every day starting at about ten A.M.—and wait for a decent gap in traffic. One of my townie friends told me that her husband once ran across a highway in Iowa, to Sizzler. When he was eight years old, his parents put him on a bus alone to visit relatives. When the relatives weren't there to pick him up, the bus station manager suggested he go to Sizzler and wait. Ultimately, it turned out that he had gotten off at the wrong stop. To this day, he has very fond memories of that all-you-can-eat buffet.

Nowadays, Madison has more to offer than a Mickey D's across a highway. It's got computer camps and tennis lessons and art programs. And I like that, because my adjustment has been a weird hybrid of my urban identity, my suburban lifestyle, and my townie baggage. I know the kinds of social diversity and cultural opportunities that kids have in big cities, and I remember what townie life is like, so my definition of parental mastery in suburbia is to keep the kids busy and keep their time structured.

A few years after we moved here, my older daughter told me she wanted to quit ballet. "Quit ballet?" I yelped. "You've been studying ballet since preschool! You were one of the most graceful toddlers at the Ansche Chesed synagogue gymnasium!"

It was getting too demanding, she insisted. And she had too many other activities, like swim team and piano lessons. My eight-year-old was telling me—Michael Chabon–style—that she was too overscheduled.

I let her quit, but I was ambivalent. To be fair, I have a hard time committing to a new brand of hand soap if I haven't gotten a personal recommendation. And parenting is even harder than buying soap. *Wait, what? I'm supposed to guide you in making a decision which will almost certainly have lifelong consequences? Awesome.*

Unlike snowshoeing or hiking through the woods, ballet isn't something you can pick up later in life. The Russians kick the dead wood out of their dance classes by first grade. Even in this country, becoming a ballerina takes years of training. You spend several hours a week at the barre just learning how to point your foot. You have to know the French word for almost every step—including over, under, beat, and cut—so that by the sixth grade, you can execute all of those French commands on the tops of your toes. *Sure, honey,* I thought. *Take a few years off. Explore some other interests. Go make lanyards in the woods if that makes sense to you. But good luck returning to ballet in middle school*

when you're already used to eating and you have no idea what glissade
means.

I devoted much of my childhood to dancing. It was one of
the only structured activities I did, in fact, unless you count the
afternoons I spent waiting for David Lee Roth or roaming around
the apple orchard. By the time I was twelve, I was performing
in a local amateur dance company, which meant getting dressed
in skintight unitards, going to the mall, and shaking my preteen
groove thing for all of the local pedophiles. It didn't bother me
that our ballet teacher rode us like miniature ponies at the state
fair; I had gone to Catholic school for eight years. That diva was
nothing compared to the plainclothes squad of nuns that patrolled
the classrooms. Still, by the time I hit puberty, it became clear
to me that I had no future as a dancer.

Reader, I'm a decent-looking person. I was blessed with a
sturdy, athletic frame that is naturally suited for activities like
digging potatoes and climbing up trees to escape British soldiers.
I couldn't pass for a member of the East German women's swim
team or anything, but I wasn't willowy, either, and in the world
of ballet, being sturdy is not a conventionally desirable trait. I
know the world of ballet is changing . . . slowly. But dig this,
dreamers: Ballet is still one of those disciplines where proportions matter. It can hardly be a coincidence that the world's
most popular ballets—including *Coppélia, A Midsummer's Night
Dream,* and *The Nutcracker*—were staged at roughly the same
time that Charles Darwin's half cousin Sir Francis Galton began
categorizing people by the circumference of their heads. Like it
or not, eugenics is still the unofficial mantra of every classical
ballet teacher who's tried to squeeze a short big-boned Irish girl
into a tiny satin tutu.

When I quit ballet, I got a job at Arby's. You want structure? Try serving prediabetic people bad sandwiches, fries, and a triangular dessert food that the corporate overlords forced us to call "pie" with a totally straight face. Supposedly in order to protect service jobs for adults earning minimum wage, they were also allowed to pay me *three dollars an hour*. Sure, that sounds fair, although I obviously had a special gift for food assembly. Nobody at the Arby's on South Park Street could drizzle crappy au jus sauce on a roast beef sammie like I could! And really, who needs an artistic hobby like ballet when you can ride your bike back and forth to work every day in a brown, garbage-stained polyester pantsuit?

My parents may dispute this recounting, among others, but my sense is that I worked at Arby's because I was a small-town kid who wanted spending money and had nothing better to do after I quit ballet, anyway. Or maybe that's what teenagers are like everywhere, if you don't structure their fucking free time. If you doubt my cynicism about that time of life, here is what I wrote—that very same summer—in my diary. I've kept it all these years, for this exact moment: *I really don't care about my future. At all.* Quick, someone call the Pulitzer committee and tell them to tee up my prize.

HAPPY MEDIUMS

When faced with real evidence that my kids are stressed and overscheduled—which has happened, even in my mastery years—I try to find compromises. I do understand the angst about busy kids. I understand that helicopter parenting is not entirely a problem invented by coastal elites who don't get out to East Hampton as often as they'd like. One solution I have embraced—to balance my townie baggage with my city nostalgia, and because boarding school isn't a thing around here—is a happy medium: sleepaway camp.

You can't send them all year long, of course. Camp is a purely summertime compromise, where nature-deficit sufferers can enjoy the great outdoors and their overprotective parents can enjoy a worry-free break. Because having teenagers supervise your kids in the woods all day is a lot like having nobody watch them at all. Plus, paddling around in canoes and bunking in rustic woodland cabins is objectively a lot like boredom. These activities give campers the kind of intense group bonding experience that many kids don't get until they go on their first religious retreat, get kidnapped by a cult, or become incarcerated.

My younger sister and brother were very into camp as kids, and they even became camp counselors in their later teenage years. I only went to sleepaway camp once. I know from reading comments about that camp on the Internet that many people remember it fondly. The converted sleeping barn was particularly popular. This surprised me a little. Because naturally, I hated it. As far as I was concerned, sleeping with a bunch of strange girls in a barn was not all that different from being orphaned and sent to a halfway house.

I did love archery, though. Already, by the age of ten, I had uncommonly strong Irish shoulders. I was also fairly anxious, and therefore highly attuned to the natural dangers around me. I understood that if the teenage counselors were to lose me in the woods—and I wasn't adopted by a pack of wolves—my bowman skills would come in handy.

The very last day, the whole camp staged a theatrical performance for the campers' families. It was some kind of dramatic reenactment of the Wisconsin frontier days. For this, we were made to wear long dresses and bonnets and talk about things like the importance of women's work. Looking back, I feel like the show was sort of a cross between a book by Laura Ingalls Wilder and the television show *The Golden Girls*. Only a lot more midwestern. And not in the slightest bit entertaining.

The only other thing I remember vividly from that camp was waking up in the middle of the night during a severe thunderstorm to comfort the homesick girl next to me. The camper dorm had no basement, which my mom would have loved. But I appointed myself as her caregiver because there were no teenagers in the barn to appropriate the role. I don't know where they were, but quite frankly, their absence did not surprise me that much. These were the same counselors, after all, who'd just read us several chapters of the bedtime classic *James and the Giant Peach*. When you're trying to get a cabin full of ten-year-old girls to sleep during a thunderstorm, what could be better than a macabre book about an abused orphan who takes refuge in a bug-infested piece of fruit?

When my kids hit sleepaway camp age, we tried it. They came home early. I hope they'll have a more positive experience than I did, eventually. For now, since I need to protect them from fast food and the woods, I just keep an eye on them at all times. And save money for the therapy bills later.

Chapter 14

DOORKNOB CONFESSIONS

BEING CLOSER TO family was a big factor in our decision to move to Wisconsin. If I was going to parent like a
juvenile probation officer—and I was—I wanted the office to
be fully staffed. Turns out, the decision to live near Moms and
Pops is actually very trendy. Despite the hyperpartisan nature
of our country, there is one thing that unites us: living near our
moms.

A few years ago, the *New York Times* reported that the median
distance Americans live from their mother is eighteen miles.
Only 20 percent of all Americans live more than a couple hours'
drive from their parents. This statistic surprised me, although I
hear anecdotal evidence of it all the time. "Abby" and her
family moved to Denver, in part, to be closer to their extended
family in the Southwest. Being close to family was a factor in
the decision to move for "Hallie," "Christopher," and "Mandy,"
too. When "Jamie" returned to Buffalo, the main reason was her
family. The other was the superiority of Wegmans grocery stores.
That sounds like a joke, but she literally said: "We have the best
supermarket. It's why Alec Baldwin's mom refused to move

from Syracuse." Since learning this about Wegmans, I sometimes wish we had just moved to Buffalo.

When "Marley" and "Hanna" moved farther away from their
families, one of the hardest adjustments—even more than the
shortage of lithium and brown rice—was the distance from their
parents and siblings. For many people, of course, living close to
family isn't desirable. Not everyone gets along with their family of
origin. We're not in touch with some members of our extended
family because, well . . . sadly, my editor won't let me share
these stories for legal reasons.

But even if your family isn't torn apart by ignorance and
whiteness, it's not always easy to live near them. Those lunatics
raised you, Reader! Everyone knows that the reason they push
your buttons is because they installed the buttons. If the issue of
living close to family was a simple one, would there be an entire
field of psychology called *family therapy*? I can't answer that,
because I studied Middle Eastern history in college and then
learned a few jokes. But my sense is no.

CULTURE SHOCK, FAMILY EDITION

As you deal with cultural adjustment writ large, you'll probably
pass through a microcosm of the same phases with your family.
Just as we had to tackle our feelings about gardening, complaining,
and free-range parenting, we had to *adjust* to living closer to
family I love my family. But after living in a big coastal city for
twenty-two years, I really had no way of knowing how much
stuff they had hoarded in their attic. Then one day, I crawled up

there looking for some ornaments and I could no longer pretend they were ready to downsize into a condo.

HONEYMOON

It's common, at first, to expect too much. The "simple and good" syndrome applies here, too. Affable togetherness! Regular babysitters! Home-cooked meals! Free Netflix! Given how often my mom came to New York—and how eager she always was to sleep in our living room on the tiny leather couch—I had reason to believe that once we lived closer, she'd pretty much clear her schedule for me, if not take up residence in my moldy basement. Hadn't my parents been patiently waiting, nigh these past twenty-two years, for me to fill their empty, lonely days? Didn't they hold on to those board games—including the ones with most of the pieces missing—in hopes that their grand-children would come over every single day to play Battleship?

Although you maybe didn't know this while you were off finding yourself in your urban mecca, your parents were back home, just trying to live their best life. Otherwise known as *their life*. My parents were happy to see us in Wisconsin. They hung out with our kids a lot, on the weekends, when they didn't already have plans. But they still worked, for money. They had appointments, with doctors and auto repair people, and seemed to feel that these appointments couldn't be changed. My mom still belongs to, like, ten different civic groups, and she has her own best friends. None of whom are me.

Don't be surprised if your parents also have a daily schedule that works better for them than for you. Like, they might say that you and the kids are welcome to come over anytime. But don't call too early in the morning. They're reading the news-paper. And doing back exercises. So, anytime in the afternoon, really, after three. Also, don't expect them to help with the kids during most of the winter, when they're out of town. Or take your pets when you go away for the weekend. They won't explain it. It's just where they draw the line.

In those early weeks and months of the Honeymoon phase, it can seem like your family will make *everything* easier. One day, for example, I rode my bike to work. During my workday, some thieving scoundrel lifted the seat right off my used bicycle. Since I had to pick up my kids at school within an hour, and had no time to jump on a bus, I decided I had three options:

a) Ride my bike home four miles without a seat, risking possible reproductive injury
b) Sit on the sidewalk and cry
c) Call my dad

I chose a messy combination of b and c. Exactly eight minutes later, he pulled up in what my siblings and I refer to as his "extremely visible" white SUV, got out, gave me a little hug, and put my bike in the back of his car. It was like déjà vu all over again.

Near the corner where my dad picked me up, there used to be a movie theater. When I was twelve, my older brother and I tried to sneak into an R-rated movie there—it was the Buck Henry film *First Family*, I believe. I wish I could tell you about it, but I never saw it; the manager caught us. He called my dad at work. We thought we were up shit creek without a paddle.

As it turned out, my dad got more angry at the theater manager, who had refused to refund our money. It was pretty cool. But I cried anyway.

I guess there's just something about being in trouble, even when you're an adult, that makes you cry and call your dad to rescue you.

JUDGMENT

So my dad was my personal chauffeur; I had him on speed dial, and I was never ever inconvenienced or homesick for New York again. And if you believe that, party people, I have land to sell you in Manhattan. Actually—even if your family is totally into you and 100 percent compliant about cat-sitting—living near to them isn't all about free rides. There is emotional baggage in that moving van of yours, Reader, and even though your closets here are much, much bigger than they were in the city, they are also cluttered with much older skeletons.

One of my favorite movies is *Home for the Holidays*, and one of my favorite parts is when Holly Hunter loses her dressy overcoat at the airport and has to dig out one of her mom's crappy old parkas, which she then wears for the duration of her visit. Unfortunately for me, I don't have a gay brother. But otherwise, I gotta say, moving back to my hometown started to feel a bit like living inside that movie. Every day. All year long.

Home for the Holidays and *Invasion of the Body Snatchers* apparently had the same screenwriter. Coincidence? I have no idea. But I love knowing that, given the plot similarities. A woman wakes up one day to find that everyone around her is angry, overbearing, and possibly delusional. Her emotional connections with loved ones feel strained. She tells her therapist they might be alien creatures. And guess what . . . she's right . . . cue blood-curdling scream!

Does that sound more like a synopsis of body snatchers or a stormy Sunday morning in the middle of winter, when you agree to attend a church craft sale with your mom and end up having lunch with eight people you don't really know, including your mom's friend with the bad knee, that lady's adult son, and his therapy dog? As you're sitting there, it dawns on you that one of the main reasons you moved to New York in the first place was literally so that you'd never again have to eat lunch in this church basement with any of these people. They're still not your friends, and it *still* smells weird in there.

When it eventually dawned on me that my hometown family reunion wasn't perfect, my judgmental feelings spewed out like projectile vomit. Like every time I drove by my high school and thought about the burnouts in the parking lot, at least one of whom I made out with simply because my mom was late and he smelled like fresh weed. Or when we went to my parents' house for dinner with my sister's family. The cousins cuddled up on the same old green leather couch where we used to watch *The Jeffersons*, which was cute, but one night when I sat down for dinner, my sister—seemingly out of nowhere, but possibly her wineglass—announced that I was sitting in *her seat*. Nobody had sent me the memo that the dining table seating arrangements of thirty-five years ago were still in effect. I really had no idea why she laid claim to that exact chair. But I'd had a bad day, too. So I kept sitting there. Just to fucking bug her.

My diplomatic husband responded to the sudden and dramatic rise in family tension by raising a newsworthy topic of distraction, like government spying, not knowing that this would launch everyone into a liberal political spiral about the imminent dangers of a fascist police state. Then the kids started bickering, and just like that, there were three generations of people sulking at the dinner table at the same time. *This is not your deluxe apartment in the sky*, I thought to myself. *This is a fuckbowl of shit.*

As the judgmental feelings well up in these moments, convincing you that you have made a terrible mistake, follow this mantra. First, don't say "fuckbowl of shit" out loud. Your mom won't appreciate that. All you need to do is get through the meal without raising any more political topics, eye-rolling at your sister for being a stereotypical younger sibling, or exploding with an irrational emotional accusation about how your parents never let you recite dinner poetry. This meal will end. If not now, then after the pie. And when it does, you can get your ass right outta your sister's lifetime chair, thank your folks for a wonderful meal, throw the kids in the car with the Tupperware and the hundred-pound bag of birdseed that your dad inexplicably got you at Costco, and drive straight back to *your own damn house.*

Grown adults behaving like children is a psychological condition known as *regression*. I think it's pretty common, and not just in my family of origin. I spoke to a young woman named "Tina" who had recently moved back to St. Louis to live with her parents. She's the former student of one of my neighbors, who connected us. Even though Tina is twenty-six, living with her parents has made her "feel like an adolescent again." "I know it's pretty normal to move back in with your parents after graduating these days," she admitted, "and I have a lot of friends who have done the same, but it's hard not to feel embarrassed about it." Regardless of the fact that she and all of her siblings are grown up, she told me, she's found herself falling back into the role of the youngest child, rolling her eyes at her parents and acting moody and needy at the same time.

Know what her parents did to resolve it? Got her a puppy. Perfect.

ADJUSTMENT

For Adjustment phase, family edition, the same guidelines apply. Your goal is to accept those family dynamics that probably aren't going to change and learn to bullshit—I mean, problem solve—your way through others. Ideally, the family bullshit will be easier to solve than the stranger bullshit, because your family members already know what a loudmouth asshole you are. They won't be surprised if you steal their pool chair. They know better than to hand you an orange flag at a crosswalk, or step in front of your car when you're in a hurry. But you haven't lived around them in many years, and having grandchildren makes everyone more hypersensitive and self-righteous. Don't get blindsided by the inevitable family quirks.

In our family unit, for example, there is a subtle yet ongoing debate over religion. Everyone knows the Midwest has a preponderance of three things: snow, alcohol, and white people. Turns out, it's also very Christian here. No offense to the good Christians of New York, but when you live in Manhattan, it's kind of easy to forget that Christianity is a big thing. In Wisconsin, something like 80 percent of people identify as Christian, which isn't a lot higher than New York. But it feels more Jesusy here.

My parents are not Bible thumpers by any stretch, but they still practice and—suffice to say—we don't.

The topic of religion mostly comes up around Christmastime, which seems to last about half a year around here. You can decorate some cookies for three bucks down at the local mall, where some seriously nice church ladies will sit patiently with your kid while she makes the *Guernica* of gingerbread. You can go see a local production of *The Nutcracker*, performed entirely by the offspring of people you know from Sunday school, at which you will say hello to approximately nine hundred familiar faces. You can attend a "Santa brunch" at a supper club, where your kids can meet an old bearded man who looks *exactly* like real white Santa Claus. A particularly popular event is Fantasy in Lights, an outdoor light show sponsored by the electrical workers' union. On weekend nights from November to January, they illuminate dozens of large structures depicting holiday scenes, like Bucky the Badger kicking the crap out of a wolverine. Why hasn't the Fantasy in Lights been shut down by the owl people or the dark-sky gang? Because it's Christmas, so fuck nature.

Mike and I do enjoy the rituals and the holiday lights. We are also afflicted with Catholic guilt from time to time, although admittedly, that can be hard to disentangle from his legal prac-tice and my obsessive-compulsive disorder. Personally, however, I am particularly afflicted by Catholic guilt at the holidays because of my parents. I love them and want them to be happy, and this gives rise to an inner conflict because I feel like they'd be happier—or at least, less worried for our spiritual stability—if we went to church more than once every few years.

We have adjusted to the inner conflict by sacrificing our children. Not in the Incan sense but like, when the kids stay over at their grandparents' house, and my parents go to church, they go too. That may sound like a raw deal to you, if you don't believe in exposing your children to religious beliefs that you rejected long ago on ethical grounds. On the other hand, life comes at you fast. And if you've ever had to ask your Catholic parents to babysit on New Year's after refusing to attend church on Christmas, you might feel differently. Try it, atheists, go ahead. I dare you.

Sometimes, it's not their celestial opinions we've had to adapt to, but their personal boundaries. In their retirement years, for example, my parents have turned into snowbirds, which is a northern-climate term for older people who spend their winters in warm places. It's a great setup for them, and I'm mostly thrilled they've chosen to retire in style. I say mostly because a smaller part of my brain, the regressed part, gets super pissy about it: *Oh okay*, so we moved our entire lives from New York to Wisconsin, and for several months a year, *you* move away and leave us in Wisconsin to freeze our asses off and pay *strangers* to babysit our kids? My adult brain steps in to remind me that our paid babysitters aren't actually strangers. Also, my mom lessens the blow by making and freezing several trays of food for us before she leaves. But I do prefer the rest of the year—when it's not winter, and they're around more, and she lets herself into my house several times a week to leave me home-cooked food that I don't have to thaw first. Just being honest.

If you think it's weird or problematic that my mom still cooks for me, well—why do you think everyone else in America lives near their moms? My mom is a great cook! At holidays, she makes and puts out plates of kolachke, a Czech pastry made of sweet dough with a dollop of fruit in the center. Mike calls them "gooey cookies," and he's crazy about them. To this day, she fills every coffee table bowl with candy: M&Ms in the Mrs. Claus tin, Sour Patch Kids in the Santa, chocolate mints in the snowman. It's just what my grandmother used to do. The kids love it. And by kids, I obviously mean me. I slam all of it down my throat at once, and wash it down with bourbon-spiked eggnog. Oh, she always has eggnog. Eggnog originally came from Europe, Reader, but I think it should be considered the official drink of Middle America. Because it wasn't until the British settled here—on plentiful stolen land, with an abundance of grain for spirits—that gluttony was truly democratized and we had a sweetened egg-and-cream-based cocktail for a whole region full of alcoholics with high cholesterol to enjoy.

I actually made up an acronym to describe my holiday eating behavior that rhymes with nog: WOG. It stands for Winter Onset Gluttony. I came up with it at nine A.M. on a weekend morning. I was sitting at the dining table in a Green Bay Packers sweat suit, eating a slice of leftover pizza for breakfast. The night before, Mike and I had gone out for seafood crepes and sangria. After that, we'd stopped by a housewarming party, where I had two glasses of vodka punch and some homemade pineapple upside-down cake. An objective outside observer—my former self in Manhattan comes to mind, for example—would have been horrified at the sight of me walking around in a loose-fitting sweat suit that said MEET ME IN THE END ZONE in block letters on the back. But my former self wasn't up to speed on the extent of my annual holiday engorgement.

Adjustment, by the way, is a two-way street. My mom is really nice about inviting me to her civic events, for example. I enjoy her close friends, many of whom I've known for most of my life. But I'm not retired yet, and if I'm not working, I sometimes prefer to stay home and take a nap underneath a cat. I don't necessarily tell my mom that, because she doesn't believe in napping. Or having cats. Instead I tell her I'm cooking dinner, because in my family, dinner is the only acceptable reason to skip lunch. At the same time, my mom doesn't want to come to all of my stuff, either. I've invited her to join me at yoga dozens of times, and every single time, she looks at me like I just poked her in the face with a burning hot stick of incense, then she says she has to cook dinner.

If you ask my kids, nobody has had to adapt at all. They love having cousins nearby. We get together pretty regularly. Their grandparents attend just about every piano recital, choir or band concert, spelling bee, and graduation ceremony. In the summer, when Mike's parents visit, we have both sets of grandparents around. It's the best kind of problem to solve because it's not a problem at all. And now that we have all gotten used to our mutual boundaries and expectations, I wouldn't trade the grandparents for admission to all the private schools in New York. Except maybe Brearley.

MASTERY

Being your true self with your family of origin can be tricky. While they've known you for your whole life, they haven't lived near you for decades. You share genes, but you don't share all the same opinions. And it takes time to reacquaint yourself with everyone's foibles. Like, my mom knows that I still hate broccoli. Why the hell does she still try to sneak it into my free food? The one thing about living near my family that never feels tricky is that—despite being utterly indifferent to our prize-winning guinea pig—they always help, to the best of their ability, when we or the kids are sick or in crisis. In those times, I never miss Manhattan. We hold family close, and let them do the same.

The crisis management goes both ways. Now that my parents are in their seventies, injuries and ailments hit them on the regular. My sister and I are both close enough to help out. For me, helping out usually means texting my sister and telling her to help out. Sometimes I go the extra mile and take a picture of the problem and text it to her for virtual diagnosis. Other times, I'm just here to listen to them. Or drive them someplace. Or visit them in recovery. And I feel lucky about that. Because I have many, many friends who have already lost their parents or worry constantly, from far away, about their failing health.

Since I'm confessing family secrets on my way out the door, however, let me also share this: When I left New York, I didn't just bring my cool handbags and sarcastic attitude. I also brought my problems. This is an important tidbit of truth, Reader, which should be scrutinized when you figure out how to leave and where to go. The flip side of *being yourself* no matter where you live is that you are also *stuck with yourself* no matter where you live. Your problems are your problems, irrespective of location. Those problems will happily travel the entire distance from Manhattan to Wisconsin, like an imaginary friend who rides atop your car.

Our second winter here, I had a nervous breakdown of sorts. I can't say it was related to moving, but I can't say it wasn't. The reasons were jumbled in my head, as they so often are when you feel anxious. It was wintertime. It was *really* cold outside. I was trying to finish an article on a tight deadline. The holidays were upon us, and I had a lot of cleaning and cooking to do before hosting my family, and my sister's extended family, for Christmas Eve. They are incredibly nice Milwaukee people, and I wanted them to feel welcome. I was bound and determined to make some tasty gluten-free lemon bars for sweet old Grandma D, and not drop any unnecessary f-bombs.

One morning, while sitting down to work, I felt chest pains. I called our local clinic, which is two minutes away, even by a really slow stagecoach, and the doctor on call told me that if I believed I might be having a heart attack, I should go straight to the emergency room. If I did *not* believe that, she said sternly, then I should stay home. It was almost the holidays and she clearly didn't want me in there. But this instruction was a classic rookie mistake, worse even than the handsome baby doctor from the ER at New York–Presbyterian. Heads up, doctors: Never give a seasoned hypochondriac the opportunity to self-diagnose. They will always take that tiny sliver of impending mortality and run with it. Could my problem have been acid reflux, an affliction suffered by others in my family? Yes. Could it have been benign heart palpitations brought on by the excessive ingestion of coffee? Oh sure. It could've been a sore shoulder, to be honest. But I couldn't really rule out a heart attack, or any number of other severe illnesses, including but not limited to pneumonia, lung cancer, or angina, whatever that is.

I drove straight to her office.

When the doctor finally came into my exam room, she said nothing for what felt like several minutes. When you believe you might be dying of a cardiovascular event, time moves very slowly. When she did finally speak, she reprimanded me for coming in against her wishes and angrily reported that now that I was here, she was obligated to order some tests. After she finished the patronizing lecture part of the exam, she ordered an EKG. Unfortunately for everyone involved, including the rookie, the results came back abnormal.

Doctor Scoldenheimer was clearly surprised. She explained— now in a very slow, soothing, guilty tone of voice—that an abnormal EKG can be perfectly normal, as long as it's *always* abnormal. I understood it thusly: An abnormal EKG is the medical equivalent of being sixteen years old, having never been to Universal Studios, and thinking that your state fair has a pretty cool amusement park. You have no baseline standard, no sense of scale. Once you finally get to Los Angeles and get more information, you realize that the state fair would've been a lot better with Butterbeer and cool rides run by talented aspiring actors rather than dirtball methheads who hit on young girls.

Since the doctor didn't have more information about the better amusement parks, however, she sent me straight to the hospital. My first impression was *wow, this is nice.* Compared to New York hospitals, which are perpetually overcrowded, it was like a hotel. Clean. Shiny. Empty. If you're admitted for a heart condition, you don't have to share a room with a homeless person passing a gallstone or a screaming girl whose mouth was wired shut, as Mike and I did, on different respective occasions, in New York. This town may have been settled by pioneers and built by progressives, but it's owned by hospitals now. The rest of us are just here to drink too much eggnog and hope someone knows what angina means.

The great thing about that day, apart from the fancy hospital room, was that my parents were there to pick up my kids at school and help out at home until Mike finished at work. The great but awkward thing about that day was that my sister was working in the hospital. Reader, I love my sister. And she's a great physician, except when she's trying to predict a menstrual cycle based on incorrect facts. But my sister, bless her heart, is no friend to hypochondriacs. In fact, the whole entire reason she wanted to work in a hospital in the first place was so she could spend her days helping people who were truly sick and never have to deal with fake state-fair patients like me.

When she walked into my hospital room to visit, she rolled her eyes. I couldn't even blame her. *I* didn't even think I was dying, and I was the fake patient! She came over to check on me and smiled. I assured her that even committed lifestyle hypochondriacs don't like spending the night in the hospital. I told her I thought I probably just had a panic attack. She agreed, but she thanked the nurses for keeping an eye on me anyway. In the morning, I had a stress test, passed it, and the hospital sent me home. My sister rolled her eyes one more time, for good measure.

Did I enjoy being my sister's fake patient? No. Did she enjoy it? Only in the very limited sense that she's been able to make fun of me ever since. But it was better than the last time I went to a hospital for a panic attack.

That time, I was still in graduate school, studying for my general exams. I was single, alone, financially strapped, and either couldn't afford to come home for the holidays or didn't want to deal with the ramifications of my mom's old puffy coat. Nothing about my mental condition felt particularly unusual back then. Mental health breakdowns are what your twenties in New York are all about, baby! I knew one guy who briefly lost his marbles and removed all his clothes outside of an off-Broadway theater. Another guy I knew threw his cell phone into the East River to evade the alien spies. The people I knew who *didn't* have panic attacks did other, self-destructive things, like marry terrible people or drop out of school. We were all exactly like Tina the millennial, only back then, our parents didn't give us puppies.

Since the school clinic was closed, I went to St. Vincent's Hospital. I can't remember what I thought would happen, exactly—medication or therapy or someone listening to my symptoms. The waiting room was full of people with severe problems, like schizophrenia and heroin withdrawal. I filled out a survey about my health history, which asked questions like whether I had friends, lived in stable housing, partied a lot, things like that. Since I was pretty young and healthy and didn't trade sex for money, I felt damn good about my answers. I was anxious, but I wasn't a complete mess!

The doctor who saw me sat at a small, empty desk in a tiny, windowless office and looked like he hadn't had a good night's sleep since the late 1980s. He reviewed the information on my survey for several minutes. He didn't roll his eyes at me. But he didn't smile, either, and he definitely wasn't my sister. When he finished reading, he looked up and all he said was: "So, how long have you been an alcoholic?" Then he gave me no medication, and I left, feeling even worse. This sucks, I thought. I'm still crazy, and now I also have a drinking problem?

I got therapy. I went to therapy for about nine years, off and on, and managed periods of depression and anxiety through various breakups, the never-ending graduate school, the broken limbs, 9/11, and a couple electrical blackouts. I joke about failing, but I'm truly not sure how I managed it sometimes. I'm not sure how anyone does. Remember that New York neighbor of ours, with the nanny and the driver and the kids who got admitted to Brearley? The one who almost singlehandedly convinced me— at my tipping point—to leave New York? Mike heard through the grapevine recently that she left New York. Her kids had some problems, her job was too much, and they moved out to the suburbs. Misery supposedly loves company, but I was just glad to hear that she's managing.

When I look back, I think those years might have been a little easier if I'd had some family in the area. Good things came from the hardships: I was finding myself. Falling in love. Following my heart. But finding yourself isn't just a romantic chronicle of struggling to achieve your dreams. It's also an uncomfortable process of learning that you are imperfect and have serious problems that you might have to cope with for a long time, and possibly forever.

Like I always say, Reader: Life is an adventure! And a punch in the face. And those things are true no matter where you live, or how you leave.

AFTERWORD

Many Americans don't have the privilege or the freedom to move. The world over, people are constrained by financial hardship, war, despotism, and myriad other barriers. I know how lucky I am, privileged with choices and the ability to write about them in an ironic, comedic, and lighthearted way. Especially now, in these times.

I wrote this book to help you leave a place you love and make a home somewhere else. With some universal stories, some fairly absurd reasoning, and some of what I laughingly call my "expertise," I hope I've convinced you that it is possible to upend your life and start fresh in a new place. No matter what that new world throws at you—a manic love of pie, congenital smiling, fashion clogs—you can handle it. The key to a successful adjustment is remembering that there is no *perfect* place. Every individual has to decide what she can live with, and what she can't live without.

There are glimmers of perfection. As novelist Jane Jensen wrote, we are granted "perfect moments." Like when you have a great Sunday meal with your parents, play a funny game of charades with all the grandkids, and think back to so many lonely Sunday nights in the city. In the end, adjusting to *anyplace* doesn't mean you will love everything about it. Stay true to yourself, and derive comfort from knowing that you are essentially the same person—the cool one, the loud one, the crazy one—wherever you go. Then find ways to make that place work for you.

I've said some salty things about Wisconsin—and New York, for that matter—in this book. Most were comic exaggerations and personal emotional projections rather than statements of fact or universal criticism. The memoir stuff is all *basically* true. I conflated some stories and contorted some accounts and changed some names. But the feelings are all real: I don't love driving by that same damn Arby's. I rarely shop at any of the 134 nearby Targets. Mike will never love the frigid winters. I will always miss shellfish. I have some very bad days here, when I feel pathetic and stuck, like my life has gone exactly nowhere and my time on this earth has been wasted. This often happens when someone asks for my address, and I accidentally give them my parents' address, like I never even left. I suppose everyone feels that way sometimes. But I take pride in the fact that I have never gotten mauled by those nasty geese, and sometimes, I even walk the dog at night.

One day, we might move back to New York. We miss its diversity, energy, and creativity. Or maybe we'll move someplace else, when our kids are grown and leave us, or the village menfolk run me out for being a witch, or I get old and infirm and have to spend my last days in a retirement village, drinking warm milk and kicking Mike's ass at Scrabble. Until then, we will continue to seek out the perfect moments and be our best true selves. Because family is important, and for now, that trade-off works.

One day last summer, I was sitting with my dad on my parents' back porch. As we watched my kids in the backyard, my dad told me, with misty tears in his eyes, that these years with all of the grandchildren have been some of the happiest of their lives. I still don't like iced tea. But I was glad to be on that porch, nevertheless.

ACKNOWLEDGMENTS

I don't have a gratitude journal, but I have plenty of gratitude.

Lea Beresford, my editor at Bloomsbury, utterly transformed this book through her critical insight and creative vision. Editing is a painstaking and sometimes painful process for authors; Lea's superb editorial instincts made it easy and enjoyable. I am indebted to publisher Cindy Loh, for giving me the opportunity to work with these incredible professionals. Thank you to Laura Phillips, head of managing editorial, and managing editors Jenna Dutton and Sara Kitchen, for patiently guiding me through the publishing maze. I appreciate the contributions of Bloomsbury's entire team: editorial director Nancy Miller, publicity director Marie Coolman, publicist Lauren Hill, publicity assistant Rayshma Arjune, marketing director Laura Keefe, marketing assistant Ellen Whitaker, copy editor Rita Madrigal, art department director Patti Ratchford, jacket artist Tree Abraham, head of sales Cristina Gilbert, subrights professional Jennifer Kelaher, and publisher's assistant Muse Ossè. Finally, thanks to the superstars at Audible, for turning this narrative dream into a reality for people who read with their ears.

My agent, Yfat Reiss Gendell, believed in me before anyone else in the industry did. If I were only grateful for that, my gratitude would be overflowing. But it still wouldn't be enough, because she's also a marvelous agent, fierce businesswoman, and lovable lady, and there's simply nobody I'd rather have representing me to the real world. The rest of the Foundry team also moves mountains. Thanks to editorial associate Jessica Felleman, controller Sara DeNobrega, assistant controller Colette Grecco, foreign rights director Kirsten Neuhaus, foreign rights assistant Heidi Gall, director of filmed entertainment Richie Kern, and filmed entertainment assistant Molly Gendell.

Outside of the literary world, a vast network of friends and acquaintances helped me to create this narrative. Thank you to everyone who shared their stories about moving. Your book names are Ruby, Hillary, Mandy, Jamie, Hope, Reilly, Hallie, Cara, Laura, Abby, Christopher, Hilde, James and Kaia, Marley, Frank, Lina, Hanna, and Tina—but your real experiences helped to universalize and enrich this project, and I truly appreciate your time and thoughtful responses to my questions. To Hanna, my first real writing partner, I'm so glad we did that. And to Marley, who admired my leopard print shoes years ago at a writers conference, then became my friend, offered to read some pages, and assured me "there was definitely a book in there," everyone needs a brilliant mentor, and I'm straight blessed that you're mine.

Many individuals appear in this book as themselves—Tara, Justine, Michelle, Cheryl, Mark, Jenni, Jill, Bob, Helen, Dio, Alfredo, Luke, and all the DCAS crew—and I'm grateful for both the historical relationships and the enduring friendships. An extra bit of thanks to Tara, for literally always being there, and Justine, who started the blog that ultimately turned into this book, for sharing her incredible talent with me.

Among those many people who offered advice through the many years it took to tame my inner writing beast, I'd like to thank Nina Totenberg, Art Silverman, Caryl Owen, Martha Hodes, Robin Kelley, Anne Strainchamps, Steve Paulson, Linda Falkenstein, Shannon Kleiber, Christi Clancy, Doug Dorst, Ann Imig, Erik Johnson, Alisyn Camerota, Victor Cruz, Jordan Ellenberg, Karen Karbo, Alicia Ybarbo Zimmerman, Mary Ann Zoellner, Elissa Bassist, Andrew Kaye, Eileen Lavelle, and Laurie Scheer. For other forms of personal support and thought inspiration related to this manuscript, thank you to Alivia Gilbert, Fermina Gutierrez, Jeanne Evans, Renata Bauman, Martha White, Cara Faris, Kathy Muranaka George, Deb Johnson Nies, Kamille Adamany, Angie Ferguson, Jake Salzman, Sarah Bickers, Scott McKinney, and last but not least, Amy Chaffee and all the thundercunts, our merry online band of pranksters, who got me through some very dark days at the (ahem) end of 2016. You remain, in my virtual and actual heart, a fantastic rainbow of all that is swell.

I am fortunate to have a loving and supportive family, on both sides of the aisle. Big thanks to my awesome siblings, for helping me professionally, and being so much f-bomb fun. To my parents, Bill and Connie: Thank you for funding most of my existence, even when I was in college and called you bourgeois sellouts. Thank you for teaching me so much about psychology and law and feminism and parenting. Thank you for letting me move away, and helping us to come back. Sorry we haven't gotten that railing on our front steps yet. Soon.

My greatest honor and challenge in life has been raising two brilliant daughters. They are the main reason I started writing, and they appear in much of my storytelling. But their own narratives, both lived and written, will be far more exquisite than anything I could ever produce. As for Mike, who helps me to be a better person every day, through his quiet patience and wisdom and perseverance and composure, even when I'm writing personal stuff about him in public, thanks for being my best friend. You've taught me so much, and I love you.

A NOTE ON THE AUTHOR

ERIN CLUNE is a journalist and comedic writer whose work is regularly featured on NPR's *All Things Considered*, PRI's *To the Best of Our Knowledge*, and in *Medium*, the *Rumpus*, and many other media outlets where information meets funny. She is also the co-author (along with *Today* show producers Alicia Ybarbo and Mary Ann Zoellner) of *Sh★tty Mom for All Seasons*. Erin lives in Madison, Wisconsin, with two kids, two cats, one husband, one dog, one guinea pig, and zero doormen.